CASTLES
AND
PALACES

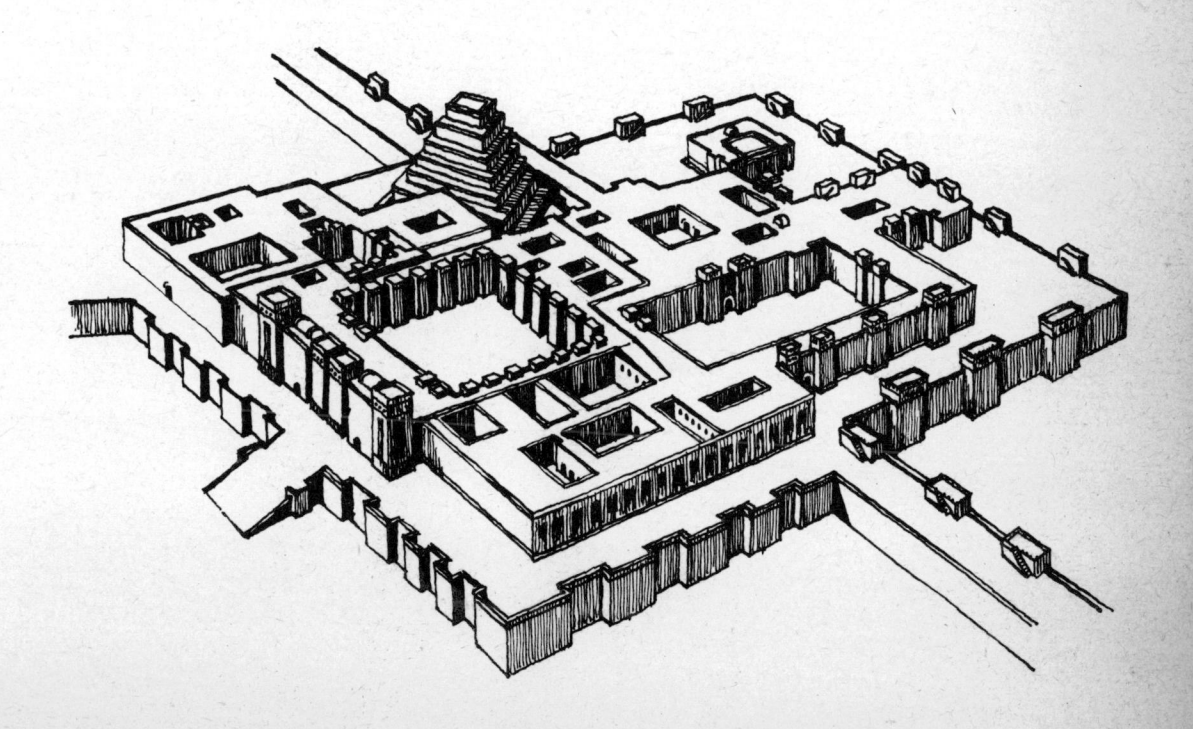

CASTLES AND PALACES — Prehistoric Britain

The walls of the village or city gave spiritual protection and sheltered the lives and possessions of the inhabitants. The early British settlements such as Glastonbury Lake Village and the Iron Age (500–54 B.C.) hillfort Maiden Castle were built to safeguard those living within from outside attack. Maiden Castle consisted of an immense mound, or barrow, surrounded by a line of ditches with steep ramparts and protected entrances. The ramparts were protected with palisades, and the ditch bottoms by sharpened stakes. Within the earthworks were groups of circular huts, as at Glastonbury, storage areas and shelter for livestock. The major weapon of the time was the sling. The castle defences were not broken through until the Romans, with their new and more advanced weapons, finally stormed the castle in A.D. 45–50.

The Scottish strongholds, the brochs, were built as fortified homesteads by the Picts some 2000 years ago. Built of dry-stone walling, these massive round towers stood above walled courtyards in which there were huts.

The Iron Age earthworks of Maiden Castle hillfort, near Dorchester, England. Several lines of defence were constructed with ditches 2–3 metres deep and 21 metres wide.

Dry-stone Scottish broch or castle. They were usually surrounded by deep ditches.

Typical iron age hut as found at Glastonbury

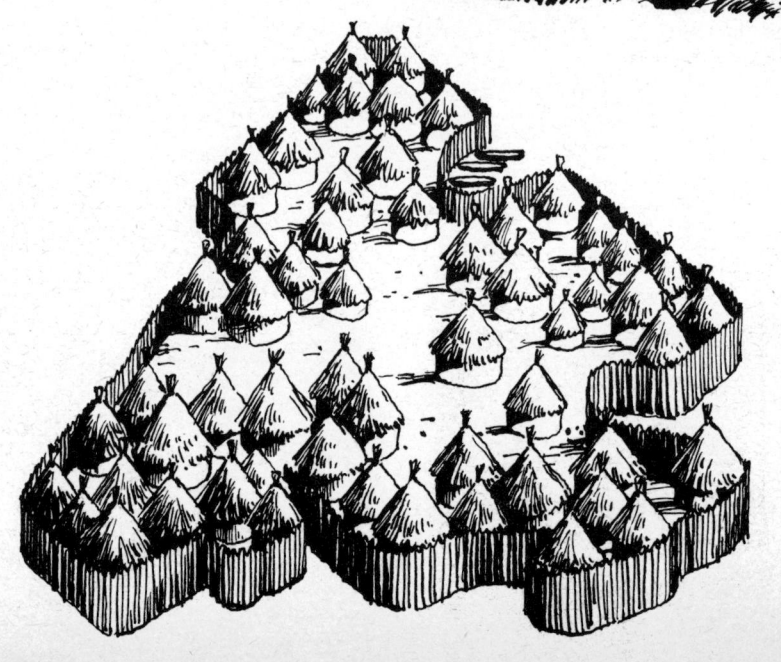

Glastonbury Lake Village

CASTLES AND PALACES — Ancient Near East

Some two hundred years before the Iron Age Britons began to dig the ditches and fashion the earthworks around Maiden Castle, the Assyrians had already built elaborate palaces on raised platforms for their warrior kings. These palaces were built by captive slaves. Sometimes as many as 10 000 were employed, working for 12 years or more. The Assyrians were fighters and sportsmen rather than traders. Their leaders were military men, and the Assyrians remained a great military power in western Asia until they were conquered by the Persians in the 6th century B.C.

The Palace of Persepolis (5th century B.C.) is a development by the Persians of the raised platform used by the Assyrians. It is a remarkable structure 457 metres by 30 metres and over 12 metres high. It is partly hewn out of solid rock and partly built up of large blocks of local stone. On the platform stood a series of elegant buildings, including the Propylaea, which formed a monumental entrance, the Hall of Xerxes and the Hall of a Hundred Columns.

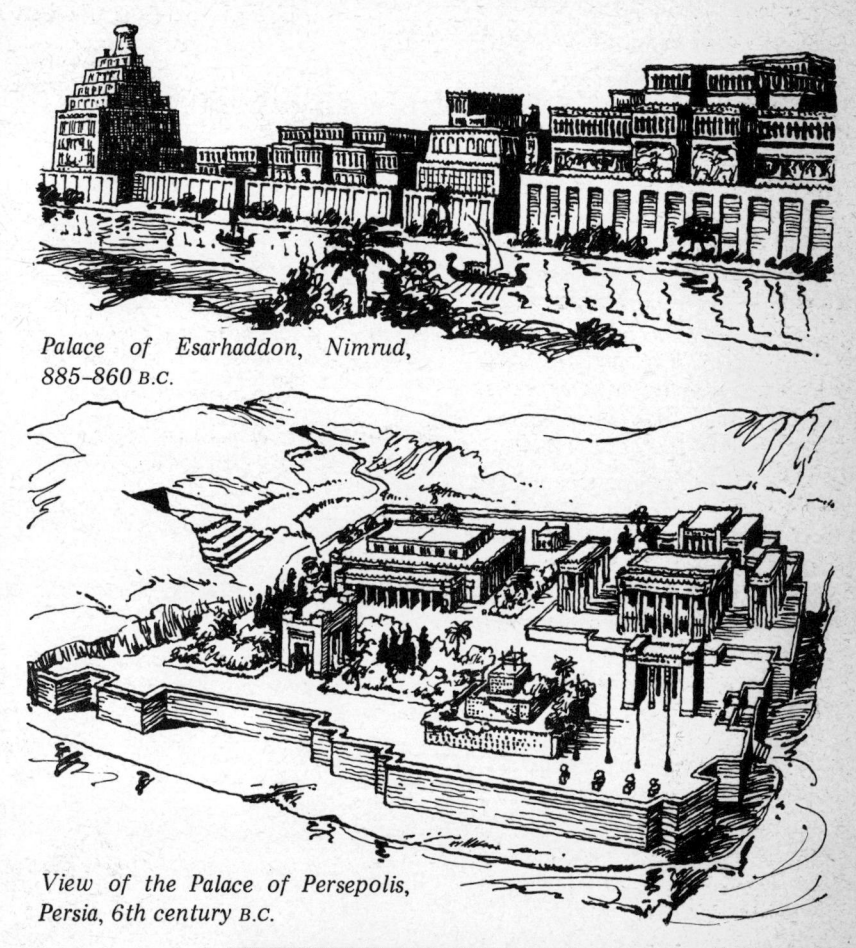

Palace of Esarhaddon, Nimrud, 885–860 B.C.

View of the Palace of Persepolis, Persia, 6th century B.C.

Hypostyle Hall of Xerxes, Persepolis

Hall of the Hundred Columns, Persepolis 521–485 B.C.

CASTLES AND PALACES — Ancient Near East

The greatest military architecture before the birth of Christ was built by Egyptian kings to secure control of Lower Nubia. Most of these fortresses, built between 2130 and 1580 B.C., were on the west bank of the Nile. The headquarters, Buhen, was the largest stronghold. Its walls were over 4.5 metres thick and 9 metres high. It had projecting towers, and a large ditch 7 metres deep and 9 metres wide surrounded the fort.

Apart from Egypt, the main centres of city life in the Near East were, at first, in southern and central Mesopotamia. Later, they spread along the valleys of the Tigris and Euphrates Rivers into Assyria and Syria. Most cities in the ancient Near East had temples. Many of them were fortified. Most were raised on mud brick platforms, dominating the surrounding city, as did the later Assyrian palaces, like that at Sargon, Khorsabad.

The buildings of the Persian Empire (546 B.C.–A.D. 641) illustrated here are very similar in structure and detail to the great baths of Imperial Rome built in the 3rd century A.D. All these buildings in the Near East were symbols of the splendour and might of powerful individuals and the state rather than a reflection of the daily activities of the people. The fortified villages of southern Morocco were another story.

Plan and elevation of the inner stronghold, Buhen. It was built by the Egyptians between 2130 and 1580 B.C.

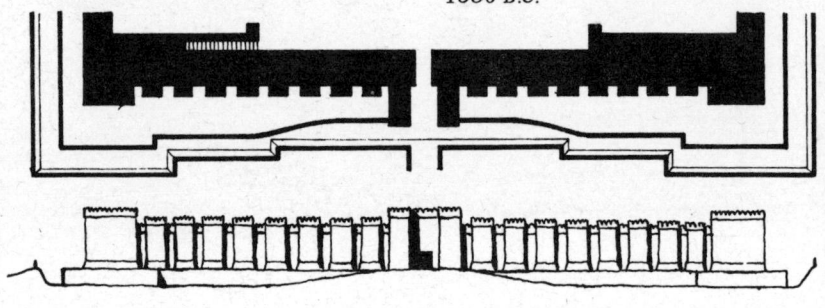

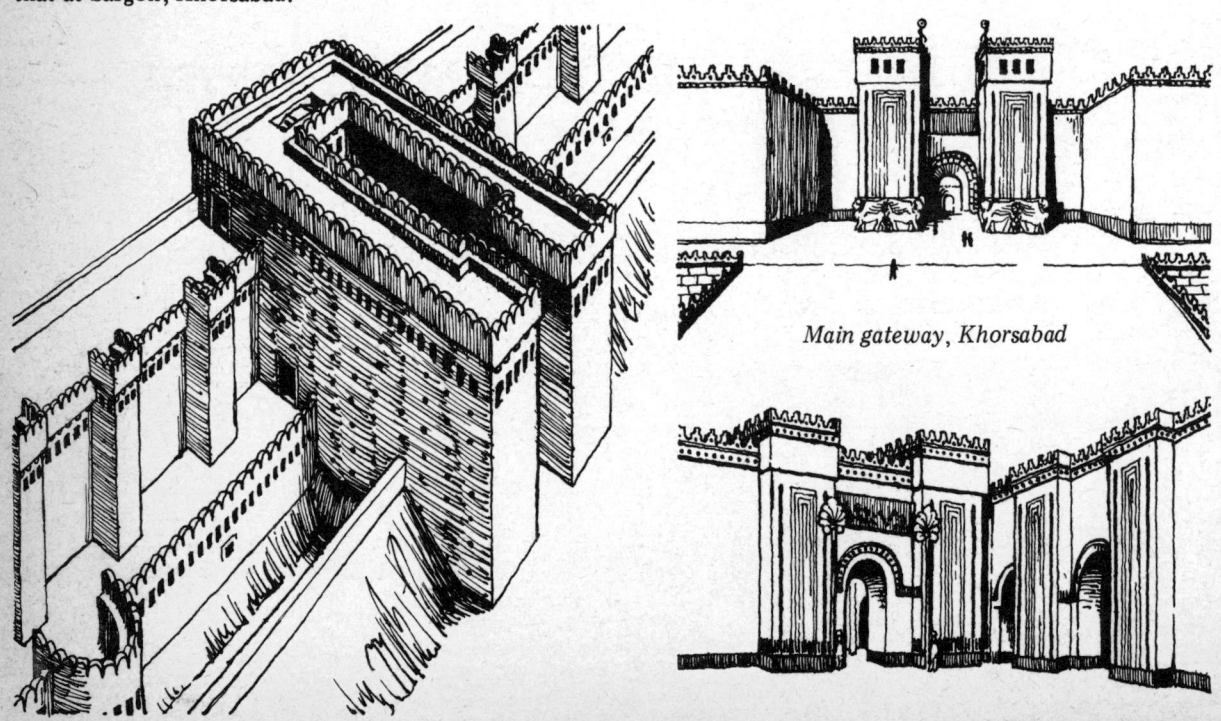

Reconstruction of the West Gate at Buhen

Main gateway, Khorsabad

Temple Court, Khorsabad

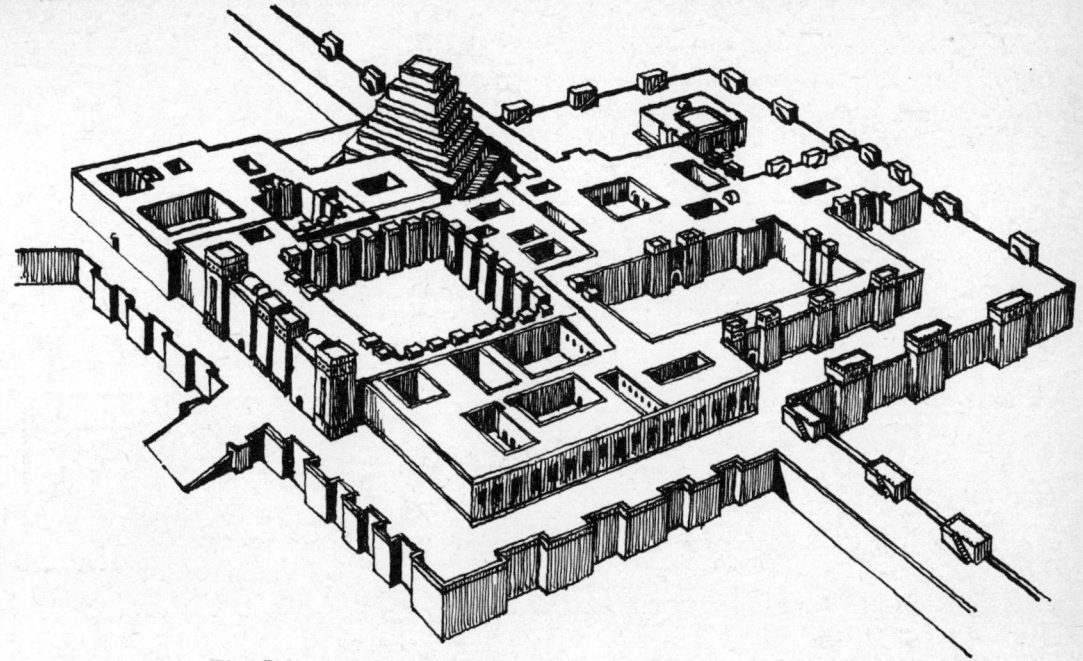

The Palace at Sargon, Khorsabad, 722–705 B.C. Built on a large platform, it dominated the city. It was a complex of large and small courts, corridors, and rooms, and covered 9 hectares.

Palace at Feruz-Abad, built south of Persepolis in A.D. 250

View of the ruins of the palace at Ctesiphon, A.D. 531–579. The structure and detail are very similar to those of the great baths of Imperial Rome.

Palace at Savistan, A.D. 350

CASTLES AND PALACES Ancient Near East

A characteristic of the stone desert between the High Atlas and Anti-Atlas Mountains in southern Morocco are the fortified villages illustrated here. Built on hilly ground along the desert trade routes, the villages sheltered and protected the caravans as they moved from the desert regions to the city of Marrakech beyond the mountains. The maze of streets within the village walls were part of the fortifications, many ending suddenly in dead-ends. The buildings were constructed mainly of mud and straw bricks, with occasional palm-trunk supports inside. The thick walls and narrow window and door openings kept out the excessive summer heat, but made the interiors dark.

The towering skyline, as we shall see, later caught the imagination of some 20th century architects. They used the same idea, but for a different purpose and with a decidedly different result. There was nothing ceremonial about the building of these fortified villages; it was a straightforward answer to a fairly pressing need—protection from both the climate and hostile tribes.

Fortified village in southern Morocco with lookout towers and protective walled courtyards

These villages dominate the stone desert in southern Morocco.

The fortified towers and walled enclosure offered protection from tribal enemies and the often hostile climate.

CASTLES AND PALACES **Ancient Far East**

Of course, not all military works were simply defensive in nature. The Great Wall of China (built 221–210 B.C.) not only kept the nomadic horsemen out, but imprisoned the peasant population inside, not unlike the Berlin Wall today. The Wall is perhaps the most famous of Chinese engineering works. Large bodies of horsemen could pass through the wall only by capturing one or more gates, demolishing the wall at some point, or by building ramps up to it, by which time reinforcements would have arrived.

The total length of the wall is 3997 kilometres. The height varies from nearly 6 metres to nearly 12 metres, and the width is 4.8 metres at the top and 9.7 metres at the bottom. The outer face has a castellated battlement. There are watch towers every 36.5 metres and fortresses at strategic points. The nearest similar construction in the West was the 22.4 kilometre long Roman Wall built in northern England by the Emperor Hadrian in A.D. 122 to keep out the Caledonian tribes.

The most remarkable defensive dwellings were the communal houses of the Hakka people. From the 3rd century A.D. onwards the Hakka people migrated from central to southern China, where they were met with hostility. As a result they built large walled, often multi-storeyed, communal buildings. In fact, they built a whole village in one building, complete with communal guest halls and ancestral halls.

Of most interest, however, is the planning of Chinese cities themselves. They were built along four basic principles: (1) walled enclosures, (2) axiality, (3) north-south orientation, and (4) the courtyard. The planning was more ceremonial than defensive in nature. The enormous scale of Peking was an example of grand planning comparable in form to the later Renaissance palaces of Europe, such as Versailles. The city itself was a work of art.

City wall, Peking

Hakka dwelling, southern China

Hakka dwelling

Hakka dwelling. From the 3rd century A.D. onwards the Hakka people migrated from central China to the southern provinces of Fukien, Kwuangtung and Kuangsi, where they built these communal villages.

CASTLES AND PALACES Ancient Far East

The model for most Chinese palaces was the Ta Ming Palace, built in the 8th century. The plan, designed symmetrically along a north-south axis, was conceived as a vast audience hall in which an emperor is enthroned. Kublai Khan's Forbidden City in Peking is a development of this.

In the Imperial Palace, Kyoto, the Japanese followed the strict symmetry of the Chinese models. The Front Hall of Audience is directly on axis with the central gate of the palace enclosure. The palace dominates the whole city.

In 16th century Japan the earthworks—stockade arrangement that characterised mobile warfare with foot soliders, archers and mounted swordsmen was replaced by the castle. This was an improved defence against firearms and cannon, introduced to Japan at this time. Built on a hill or mountainside, the castles later became the central feature around which most major cities and towns in Japan were developed. In the more remote areas of the Far East many settlements were built more like the fortified medieval hill towns of Europe, India or southern Morocco.

Ta Ming Palace, China, 8th century. Built during the T'ang Dynasty (618–907), it remained the model for later palaces.

The Front Hall of Audience, the Imperial Palace, Kyoto, Japan

Matsumoto Castle, Japan, 1582

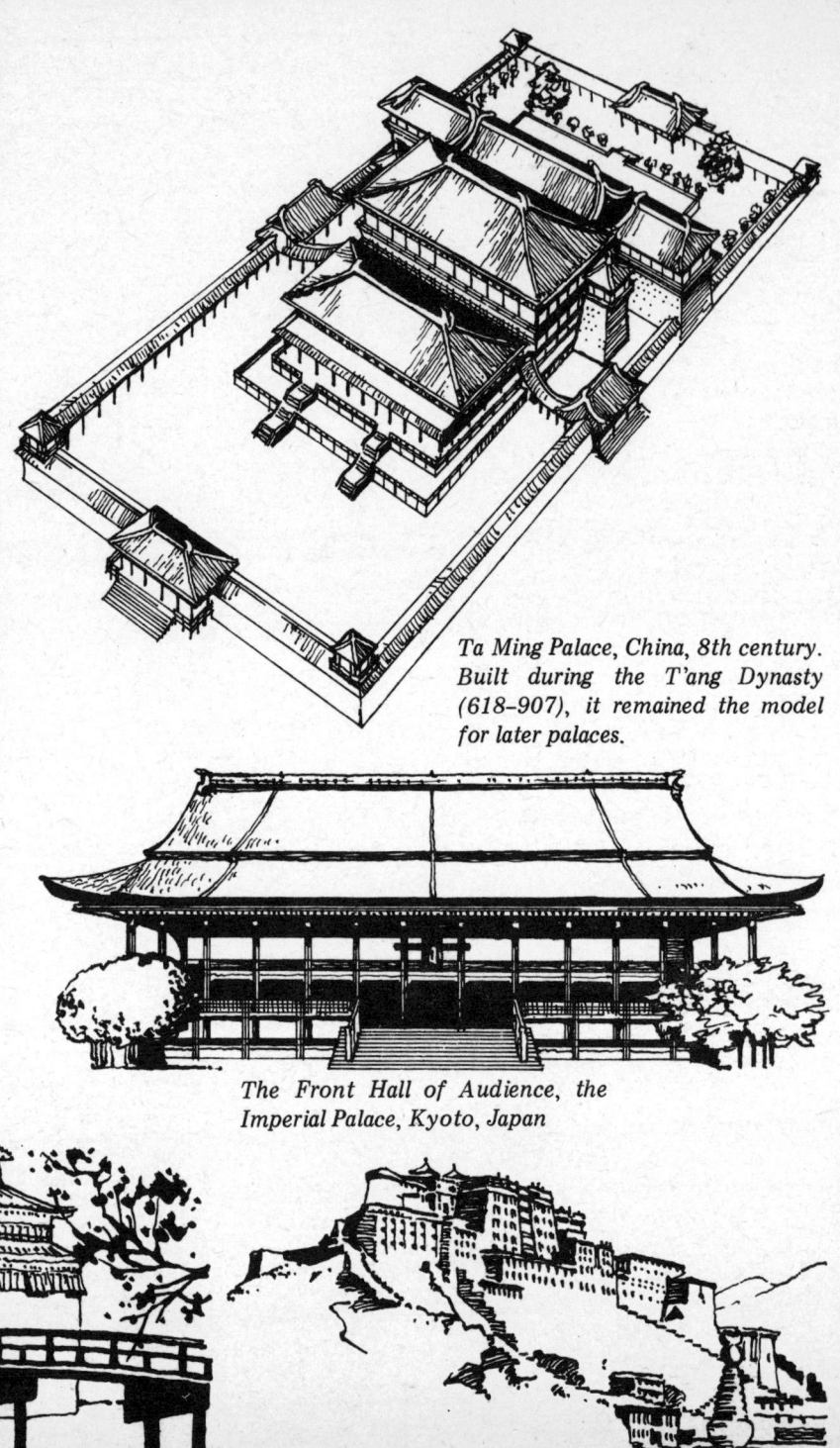

Potala Palace, Lhasa, Tibet, 1642–50

CASTLES AND PALACES Ancient Classical

On the mainland of Greece during the Bronze Age the majority of the population continued to live in defenceless villages. Several small fortified towns were built during the middle Bronze Age, about 1600 B.C. Malthi, in south-west Greece, was originally a defenceless village. The houses were grouped in a broken ring. This ring of houses was later closed when a hundred new houses were added, the backs of the houses thus forming a defensive wall.

Some three hundred years later more highly developed fortifications were built for the hilltop citadel at Tiryns (1300 B.C.). Tiryns was on the coast guarding the port of Mycenae.

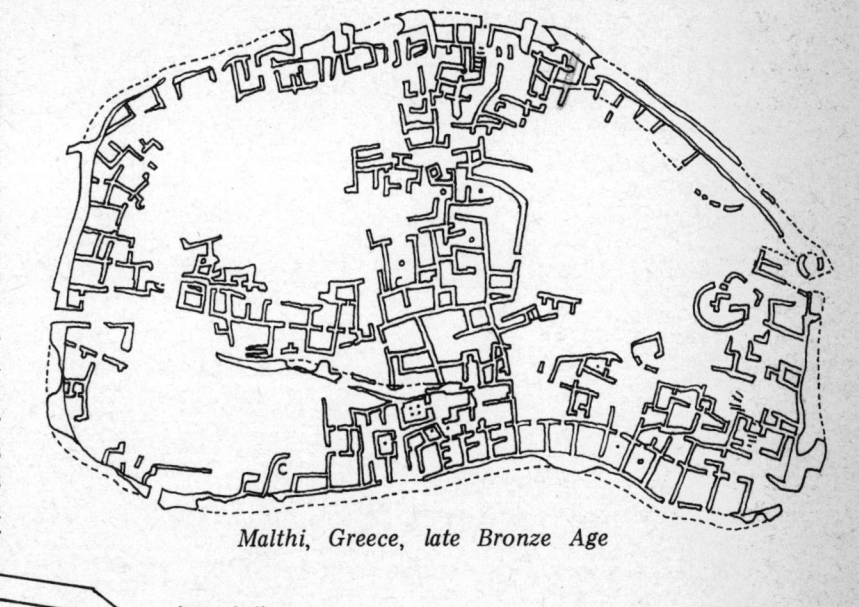

Malthi, Greece, late Bronze Age

The royal residence at Tiryns. (1300 B.C.). It is a hilltop citadel surrounded by defensive walls 7 metres thick. The palace occupies the highest part. A twisting approach to the palace was devised as a defensive measure. A cross wall divides the palace from a lower terrace, bare of buildings. This was intended as a place of refuge for the villagers and their livestock in times of war.

CASTLES AND PALACES Ancient Classical

The Cretan or Minoan period of Greece dates back to 3000 B.C. The civilisation grew and expanded, developing a commercial empire protected by a great navy that made other fortifications unnecessary. Towns grew up around small palace complexes or royal villas. By 1800 B.C. the Minoan civilisation was as powerful as those of Egypt and Mesopotamia. Knossos and other palace towns were destroyed about 1450-1400 B.C. when the naval power of the mainland princes began to dominate.

The grim fortifications of Mycenae and Tiryns are an indication of the great need for defence in the mainland centres. They were nearly all built on or near a hill. The citadel and palace of Mycenae, overlooking the inland end of the plain of Argos, were built between 1340 and 1330 B.C. Almost the entire hill was crowded with buildings. The main entrance to the citadel was the Lion Gate.

As cities developed, there was a lower town at the foot of the hill, and an acropolis, or fortified town, on the height. The word acropolis was also applied to whatever was the most defensible area, whether a heavily inhabited quarter or a fortress. By the 5th century B.C., when the Acropolis at Athens had long since lost its military importance, the citizens continued to speak of it as *polis*, 'the city'.

The citadel, Mycenae, 1400 B.C.

The Lion Gate, Mycenae, c. 1250 B.C.

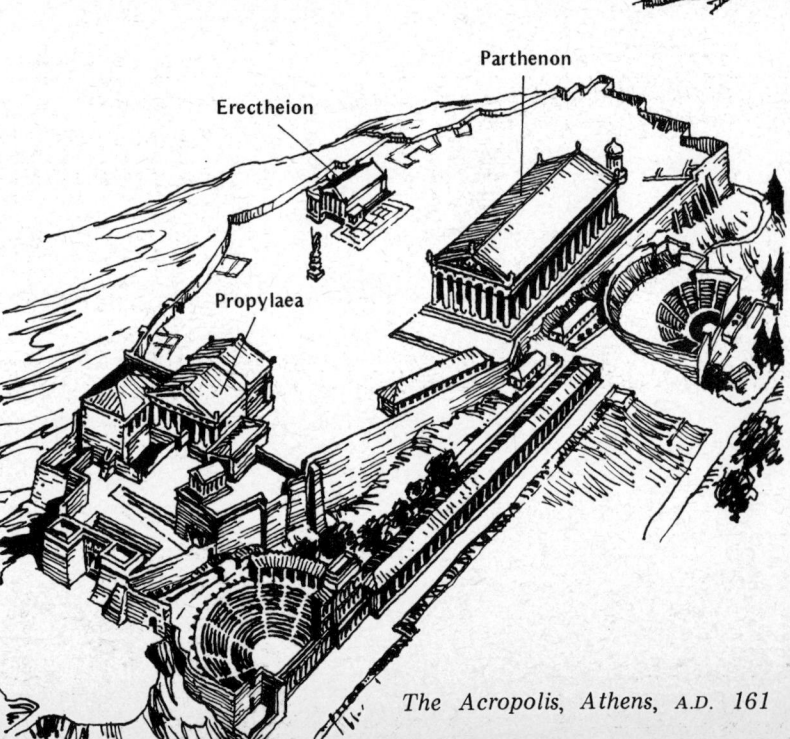

The Acropolis, Athens, A.D. 161

The main structures of the Minoan period were the palaces of the kings or local chieftains. They were quite elaborate, the largest being the palace at Knossos, home of the legendary King Minos. It was planned around a large central court. There was little need for defence since the islands were politically united as well as being protected by the powerful mercantile navy of Crete.

Mainland settlements, however, needed fortified strongholds to protect the agricultural villages that gave them a livelihood. The palaces were built within a walled citadel, as at Tiryns. The choice of a hilltop site resulted in a more compact plan to fit the narrow site. A principal room, or megaron, served by its own courtyard, was the main feature. The megaron was still used as the basis for design as late as the 4th century B.C. in the palace built at Larisa, Asia Minor.

Little Palace, Knossos

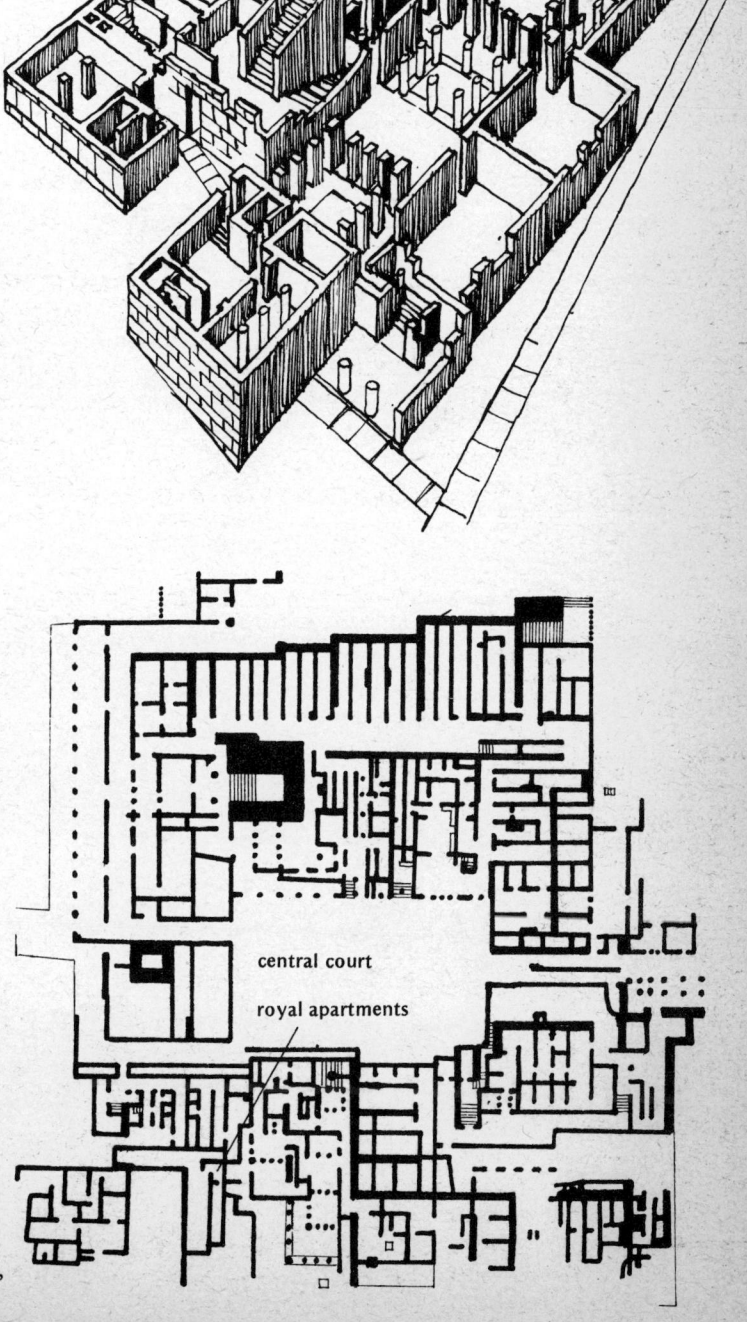

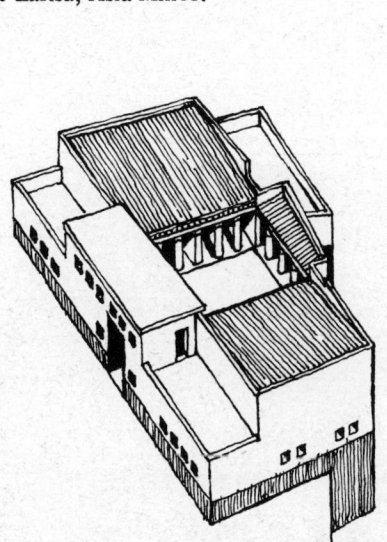

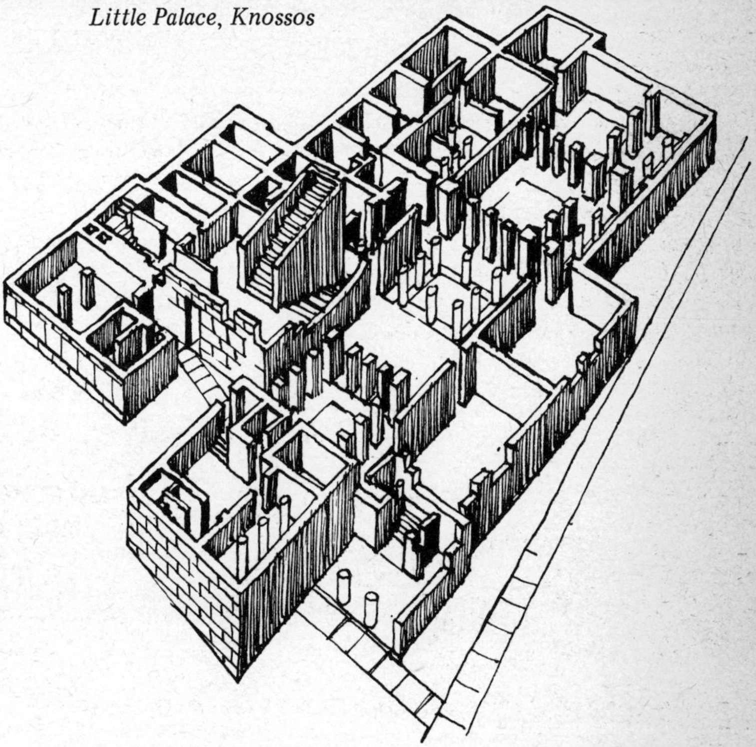

4th century palace, Larisa

Palace of King Minos, Knossos, c. 1400 B.C.

CASTLES AND PALACES Ancient Classical

The axial planning used in the ancient Chinese towns and cities had already been developed on a magnificent scale by the Romans. The Imperial Palaces in Rome were begun by Augustus in A.D. 3. The Palaces crowned the Palatine Hill and looked down on the centre of civic life in the valley below. They were approached from the Forum. The planning and siting of the various buildings was governed by axial lines. The rather strict order and logic of earlier Roman planning later had to be adapted to take account of sites with existing buildings or difficult terrain. The various angles created by the positioning of the different buildings resulted in magnificent views and irregular spaces. The introduction of various geometrical forms in these irregular spaces made the angles symmetrical and disguised the irregularity of the overall plan.

This axial planning was copied by later generations of architects and builders. It reached its most poetic form in the villa Emperor Hadrian built at Tivoli between 117 and 138 A.D. Here the rigid use of basic geometrical forms was replaced by an ever-growing inventiveness and subtlety of architectural shapes as each building grew in size and was extended over the uneven ground. The villa and its surroundings occupied about 18 square kilometres. It must have resembled a city more than a villa or country house. While the design of the building was strictly contemporary, the layout of the buildings, with their conflicting axes, stems straight from the landscaped villas of the previous century. The spirit of the individual buildings and groups of buildings belongs to an even earlier tradition, that of the wealthy late Republican villa.

The villa marks a turning point in Roman architecture. The death of Trajan in A.D. 117 marks the end of an era. Rome was at the height of its power. Trajan's successor, Hadrian, turned his back on further conquest and devoted himself to peace and sound administration. This beautiful villa is a reflection of the spirit and needs of this changing world. It was a world with a preference for the grouping of individual buildings rather than for the total coordinated design seen later at Peking, and later still at Versailles.

Plan of Hadrian's villa, Tivoli.

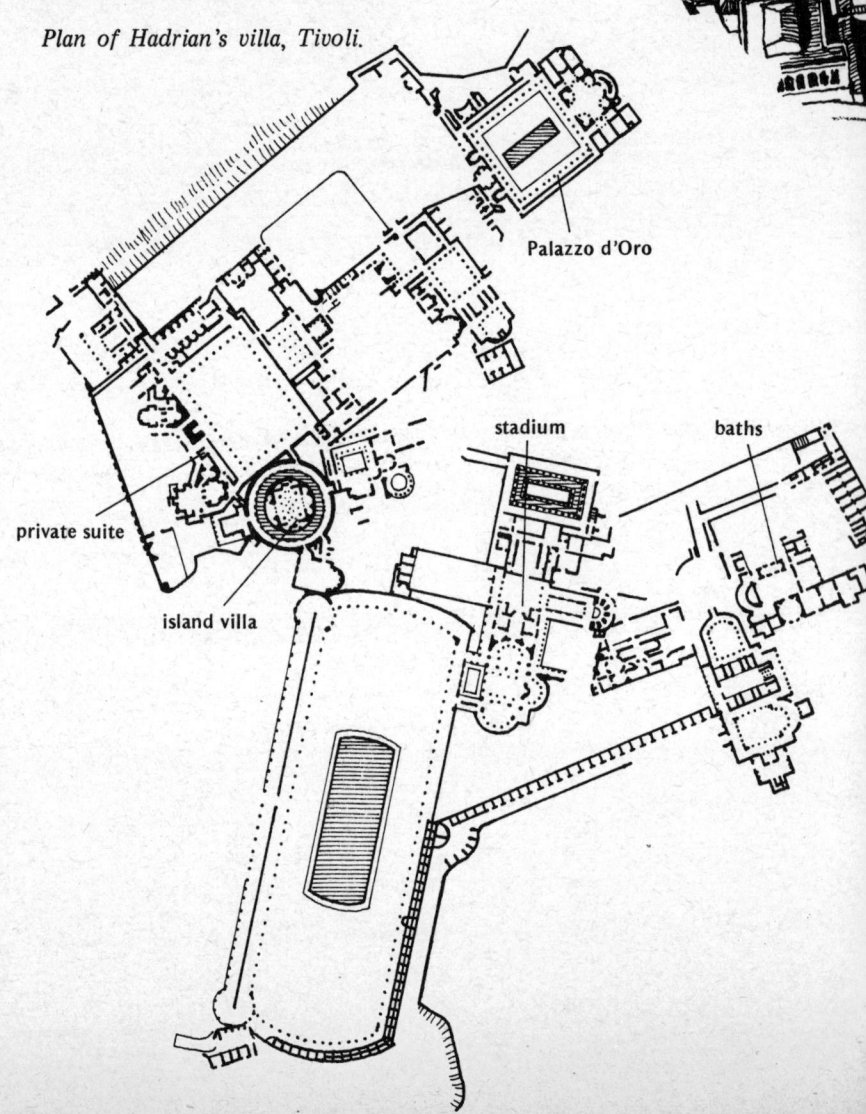

Perhaps the most obvious influence of Hadrian's Rome, with its delightful blend of sculpture, waterworks and architecture, is seen in many of the 18th century country estates of England.

Reconstruction of Hadrian's villa

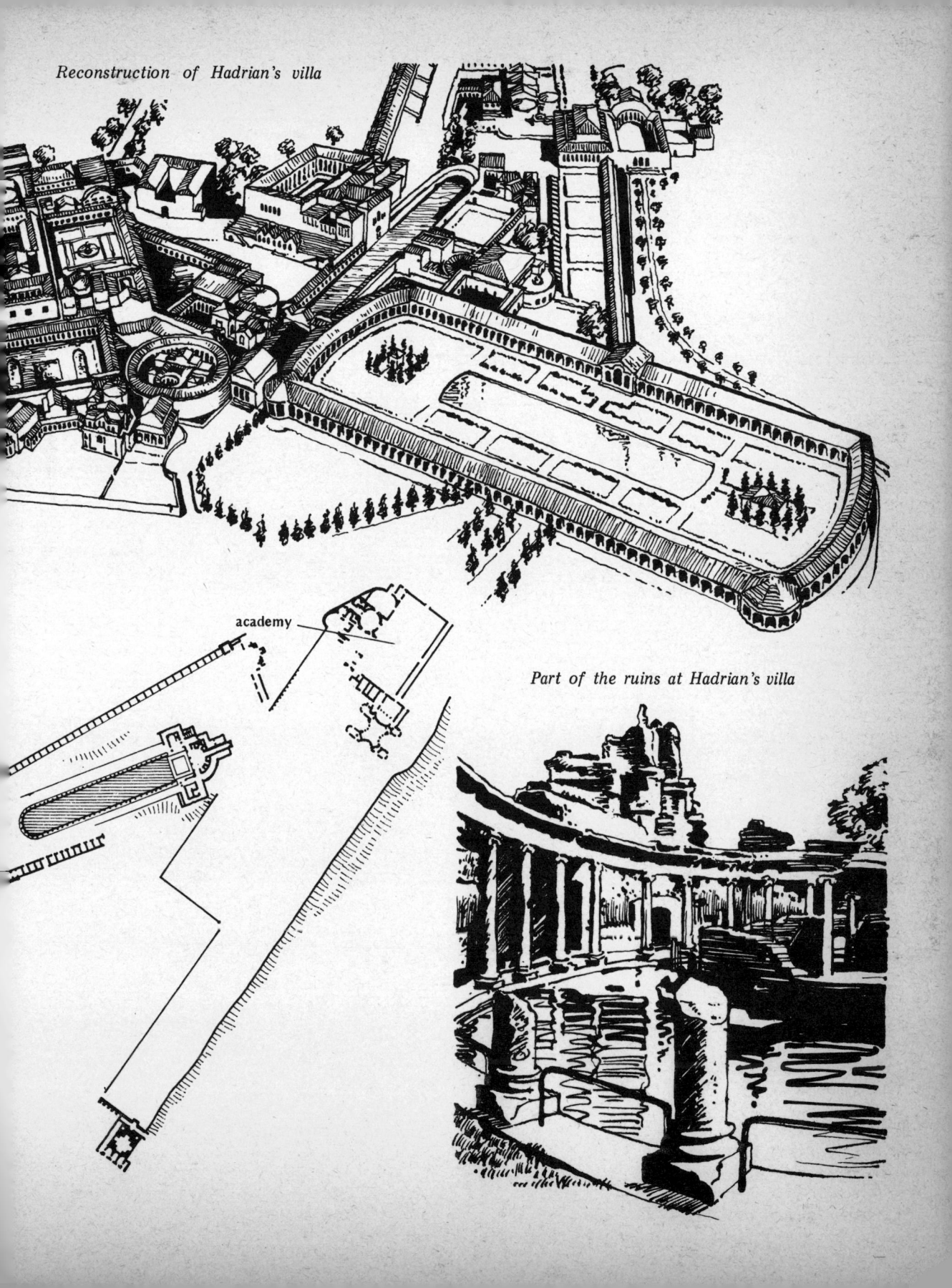

academy

Part of the ruins at Hadrian's villa

CASTLES AND PALACES   Ancient Classical

The Imperial Palaces of Rome were, in many respects, similar to the fortified city, or acropolis, of the Greeks. The Acropolis at Athens gradually became a sacred precinct. To the Romans the emperors themselves were gods, and so their palace complexes were as sacred as those of Greece. The Palace of the Emperor Augustus, the first building on the site, was fairly modest. The whole group of palaces reached monumental proportions at the hands of the Emperor Domitian (A.D. 81–96). The great vaulted audience chamber of his palace, 46 metres high, was a magnificent development of the ancient Greek megaron.

The Palace of Diocletian, built at Spoleto in A.D. 300, is based on an even earlier model. It was modelled on a legionary fortress and seems to resemble more those fortresses built along the banks of the Nile by the Egyptians between 2130 and 1580 B.C. In comparison to Hadrian's villa, Diocletian's Palace is very formal in style. Its geometry and planning are rigid.

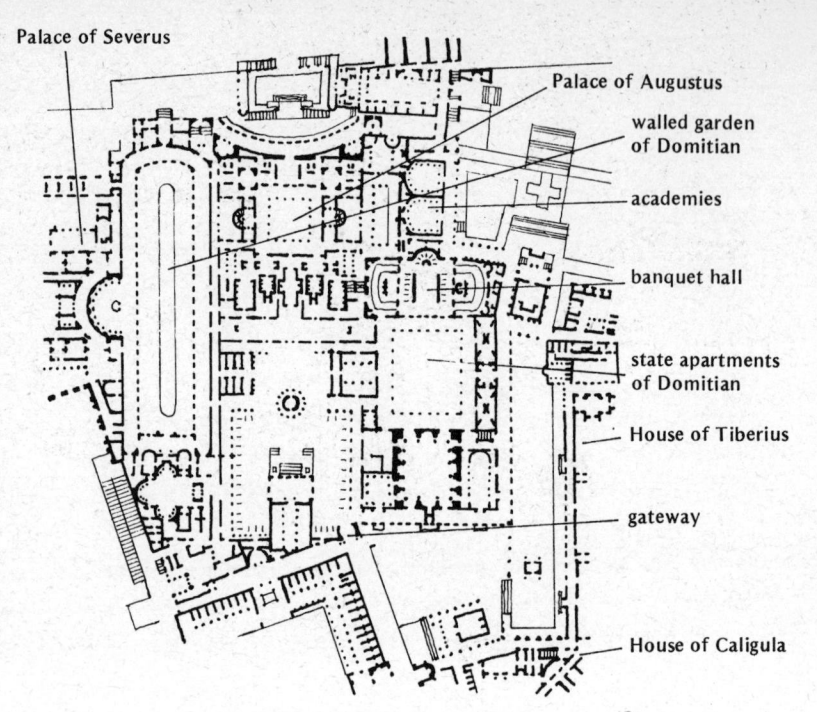

The Palaces of the Emperors on the Palatine Hill, Rome, A.D. 3–212

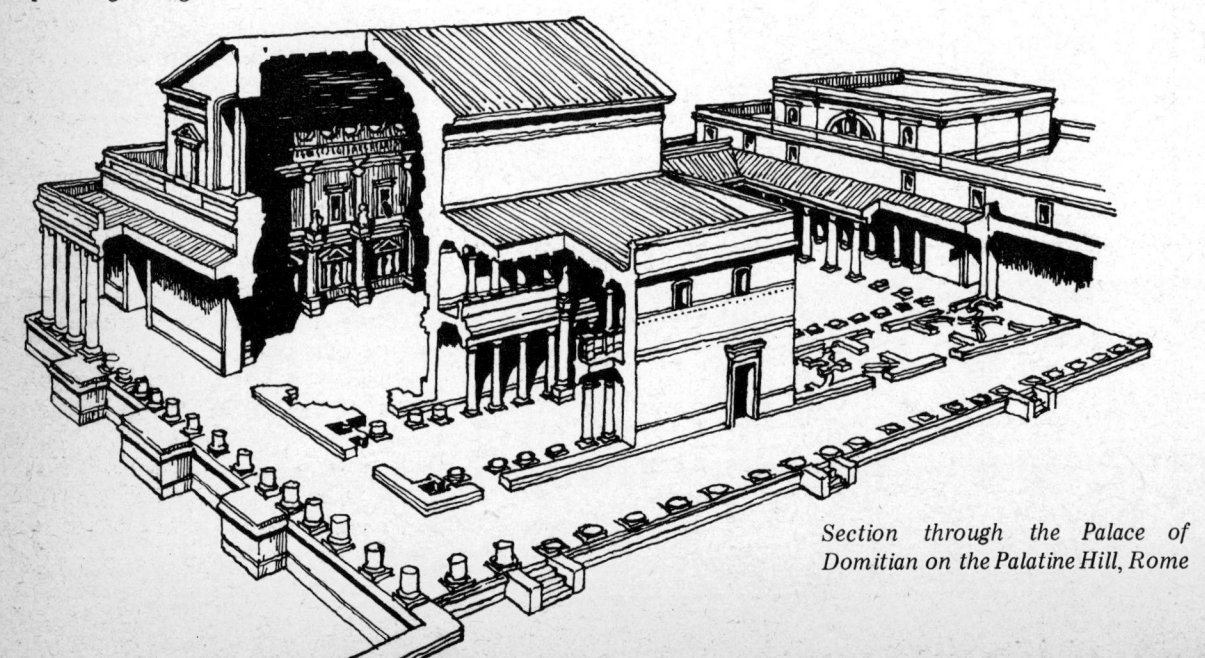

Section through the Palace of Domitian on the Palatine Hill, Rome

Palace of Diocletian, Spoleto

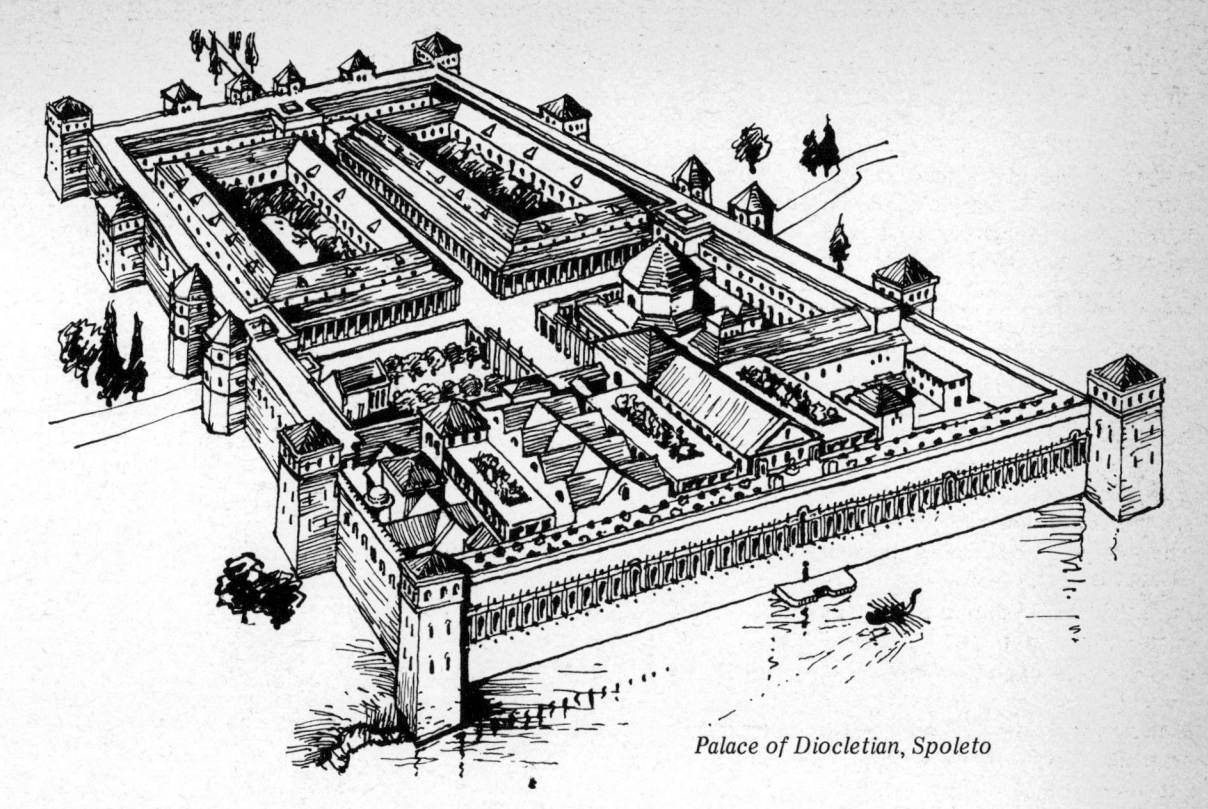

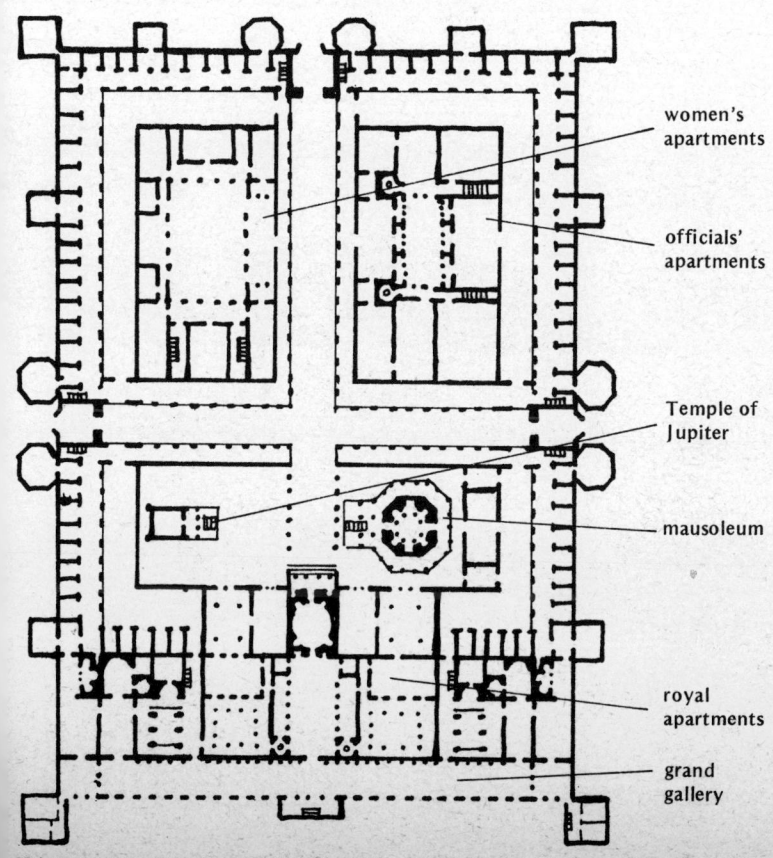

- women's apartments
- officials' apartments
- Temple of Jupiter
- mausoleum
- royal apartments
- grand gallery

Plan of the Palace of Diocletian, Spoleto. Built in A.D. 300 in what is now modern Split, Yugoslavia, it was constructed by the Emperor Diocletian as a palace for his retirement. The plan was based on that of a legionary fortress, the architecture on that of Imperial Rome. The rectangular plan covers 3 hectares. Built along the seafront of the Adriatic, it was more like a royal country house or a seaside chateau than a palace. The major feature was a grand arcaded gallery that overlooked the sea as well as connected a suite of spacious rooms. Like the later Elizabethan gallery, it probably contained works of art and was used for leisurely promenades.

CASTLES AND PALACES Ancient Classical

Military architecture is probably as old an art as religious architecture. In some of the temples and citadels of ancient Egypt and Mesopotamia the two are found combined. So much experience of fortifications had been gained by the ancient world that by 200 B.C. a school of military architecture was founded on the island of Rhodes. Other schools were opened and the results of their studies published. When the Romans conquered Greece, they came across this highly developed military architecture and adapted it to new uses.

The Roman contribution to military architecture was the castrum, or fortified camp. It was rectangular in plan, and surrounded by a rampart or a wall and beyond that by a ditch. Originally temporary in nature, this simple plan was later developed for more permanent camps or barracks. It was the model used by Diocletian for his palace at Spoleto and became the foundation for many future cities. Towers were later added to the more permanent camps.

One of the most interesting groups of fortifications was the chain of Roman forts of the Saxon Shore, built in the late 3rd century A.D. These mighty Roman forts guarded the coast of southeast Britain. There were ten forts in all, of which nine survive at Brancaster, Burgh Castle, Bradwell, Reculver, Richborough, Dover, Lympne, Pevensey and Portchester. Each could hold a substantial garrison, and was next to a harbour from which a Roman fleet could operate. There was a similar chain of forts on the other side of the Channel.

Not all Roman fortifications were based on the castrum. The burgus, or watchtower, was introduced in the middle of the 2nd century A.D. In the 4th century Roman fortress at Bürgle, West Germany, a model for later castles, the burgus acted as a sort of keep. The defence of the fortress was sector by sector. Unlike the Roman castrum, this fortress was designed solely for defence, rather than attack.

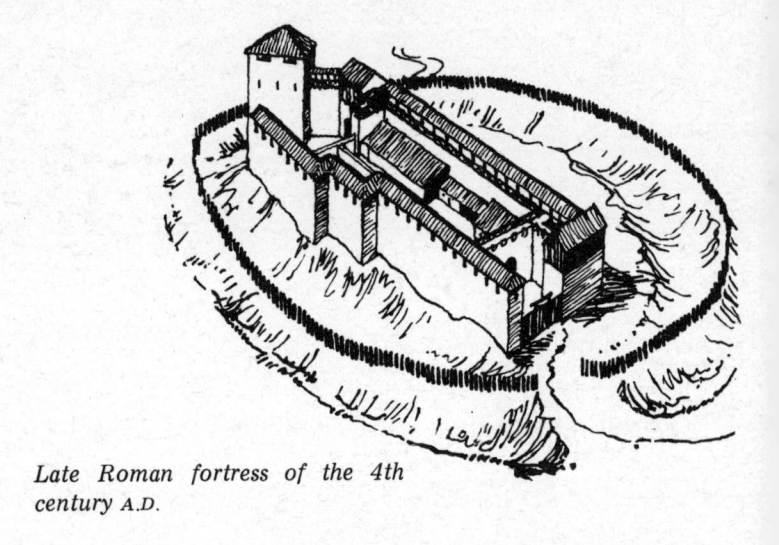

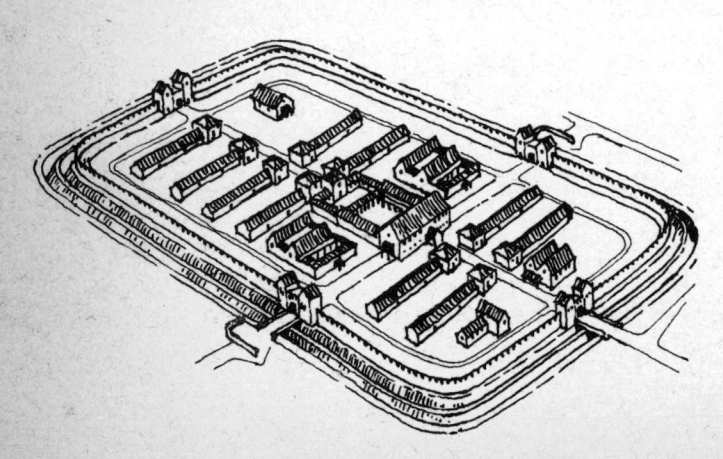

Late Roman fortress of the 4th century A.D.

Roman frontier fortress of the 2nd century A.D.

Typical Roman castrum plan. The castrum was a fortified legionary camp.

CASTLES AND PALACES Byzantine and Medieval

By the beginning of the 5th century the Roman Empire, threatened at its very heart, could no longer spare soldiers to defend the remote northern island of Britain. The famous legions that had defended the island for over four hundred years sailed from the Channel ports never to return. Many of the Roman camps formed the bases for later medieval towns and cities. Most of the Saxon Shore forts rotted away, while others were taken over by the Norman conquerors and were turned into castles. Although the term castle has been applied to certain ancient strongholds, such as Maiden Castle, Dorset, it is usually restricted to medieval buildings. Castle building began in earnest in England after the Norman conquest. Castles were originally conceived as a means of establishing a stable government. However, some became centres of oppression as well as refuges in case of hostile uprisings.

Glevum, now Gloucester, was originally a legionary fortress built in A.D. 96–98 along the banks of the River Severn.

Reconstruction of Portchester Castle as it might have appeared in 1450. Built in Hampshire, it was the last and perhaps the finest of the Saxon Shore forts.

CASTLES AND PALACES   Byzantine and Medieval

One of the four great architectural works undertaken by the Emperor Hadrian in the city of Rome was the building of a mausoleum for his imperial family. By the 9th century this mausoleum had been converted into the Castle of San Angelo by Pope Leo IV as a defence against Saracen attacks on Rome.

Most fortifications after the 5th century were developed as a cross between the 4th century Roman castle illustrated on the previous page, and an elaborate development of the Bronze Age hillforts. The castle built at Goslar, West Germany in the early 10th century is a link between the Mycenean hilltop fortresses and the motte and bailey castles developed by the Normans in the next century.

In the 10th century the terror of Western Europe were the Vikings in their longships, the Magyars, who attacked in small bands of horsemen, and the Slavs. Saxony and Germany built fortress-towns for their defence. Even the monasteries were fortified. Weak rulers found it difficult to maintain the morale and discipline of a complicated defensive system. Fortifications fell into ruins, but the peasantry still needed protection. Out of this need grew the political and military system of feudalism.

Many of these landowners lived in the earliest form of true castle, the motte and bailey. The motte was a steep-sided, flat-topped mound of earth surrounded by a ditch and surmounted by a square two-storey wooden tower. The bailey was the courtyard. Ditches were filled with water or sharpened stakes and crossed by wooden bridges, which were removed when the castle was attacked. The next development was the stone keep and curtain walls of the Norman castles.

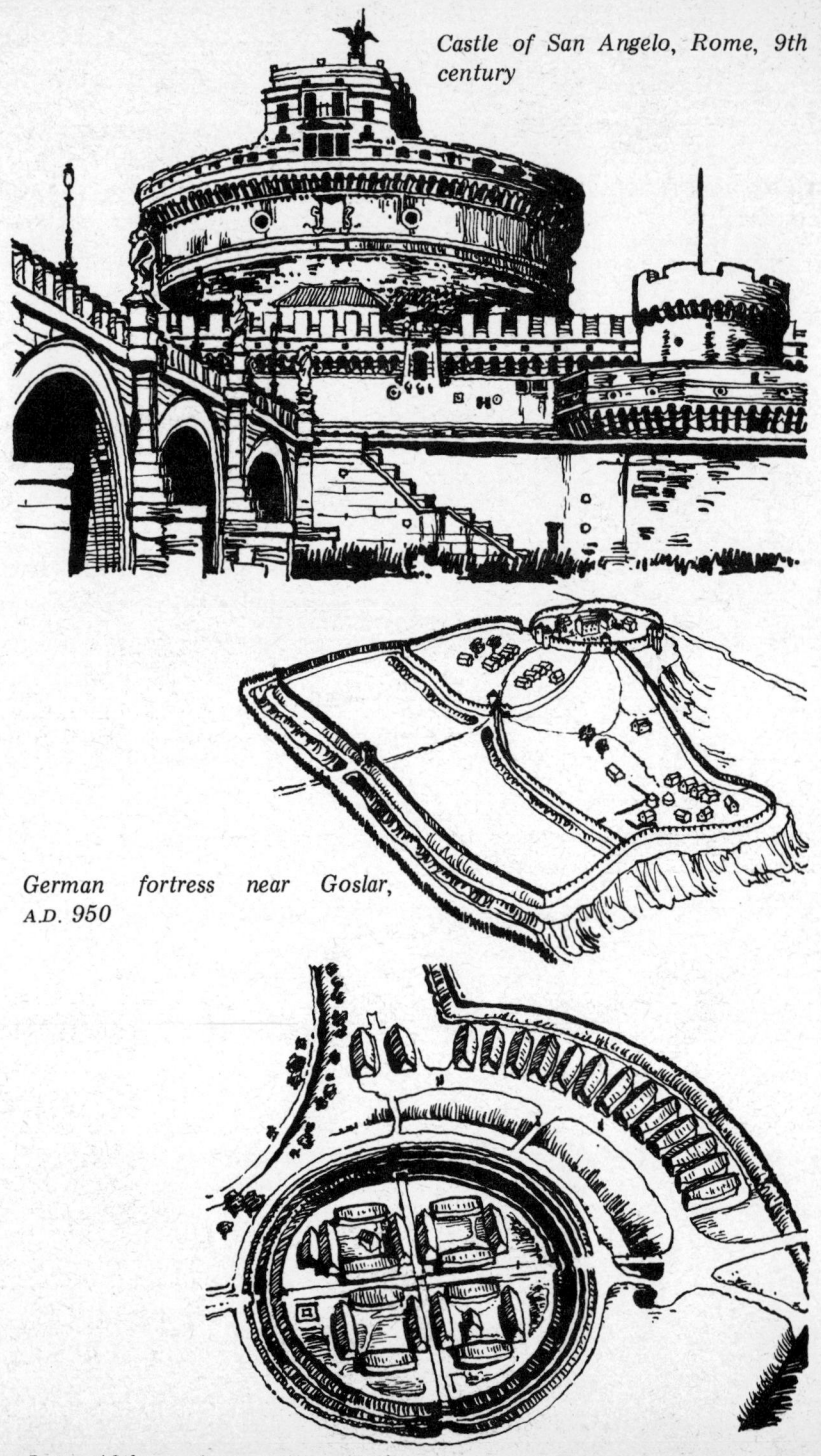

Castle of San Angelo, Rome, 9th century

German fortress near Goslar, A.D. 950

Late 10th century encampment, Trellborg, Denmark. It was a base for the conquest of England.

Fortified farmstead, West Germany, 9th century

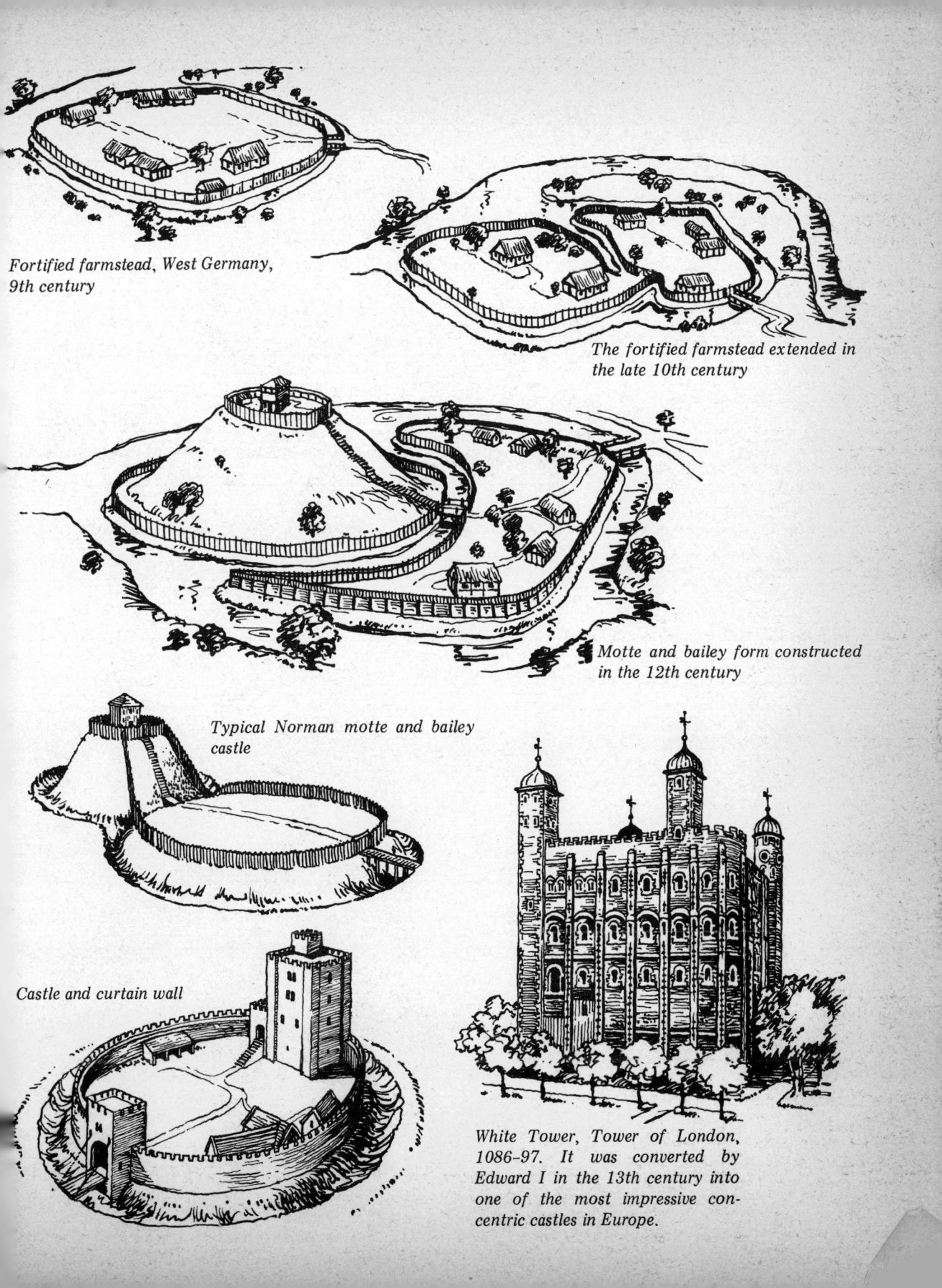

The fortified farmstead extended in the late 10th century

Motte and bailey form constructed in the 12th century

Typical Norman motte and bailey castle

Castle and curtain wall

White Tower, Tower of London, 1086–97. It was converted by Edward I in the 13th century into one of the most impressive concentric castles in Europe.

CASTLES AND PALACES Byzantine and Medieval

The motte and bailey castle was developed in the early stages of the Norman conquest of England. Later castles became less concerned with fortification and more concerned with comfort, like the one in Antwerp, Belgium. The military pressure on many castle builders was, by now, less acute. In Germany most built on land that had been in their family for centuries. They still selected naturally strong sites, often on mountain peaks, but the castle was very much a home and not a military outpost in a foreign land. Domestic buildings no longer had to be planned as part of the fortifications, but were developed much more for the owner's comfort.

The problem in Spain was very different. Here the Christians struggled to win back land from the Moors. They were forced to build numerous castles. They restored and adapted many Roman stone buildings, using the knowledge of fortifications they had gained from the Moors. One of the major works was the building of a huge curtain wall with rounded towers around the city of Avila, Spain in the 11th century. This precedes the building of the great walled towns of Europe, such as Carcassonne and Conway. The round towers of Avila were not copied in Western Europe for another hundred years. The holy war in Spain was a model for an even greater military adventure—the Crusades.

Antwerp Castle, Belgium, 10th century

Early 12th century castle built on a mountain peak

Castle at Rothenburg, West Germany, built in the late 11th century

Castle at Almeira, Spain. Founded in the 8th century, it is part of the complex of Moorish and Christian fortifications.

The Crusaders built three kinds of castles in the Holy land. (1) The pilgrim forts were sited and designed to make the routes from coastal ports to Jerusalem secure. Modelled on the ancient Roman castrum, they consisted of a thin curtain wall with corner towers, a large ditch, and an outer earth rampart. They gave shelter and security to the people travelling along the pilgrimage roads. (2) There was a great need to secure the sea links with the west, and so the coastal ports were either protected by a castle or the town itself was fortified. (3) The greatest Crusader fortifications were the inland castles, such as Krak of the Knights, built to protect the coast road or safeguard the mountain passes. Krak of the Knights was one of a chain of five castles. An elaborate system of communication between each castle was developed by means of visual signalling and carrier pigeons. The early Crusader castles were relatively simple in form and were built to assist in the capture of the Muslim-held territory. Later, more elaborate castles were built to hold the land secure. These were what is known as concentric castles. By this time, the 13th century, archery had become more important in defence, so many towers were projected outwards to give a clear line of fire along adjacent walls.

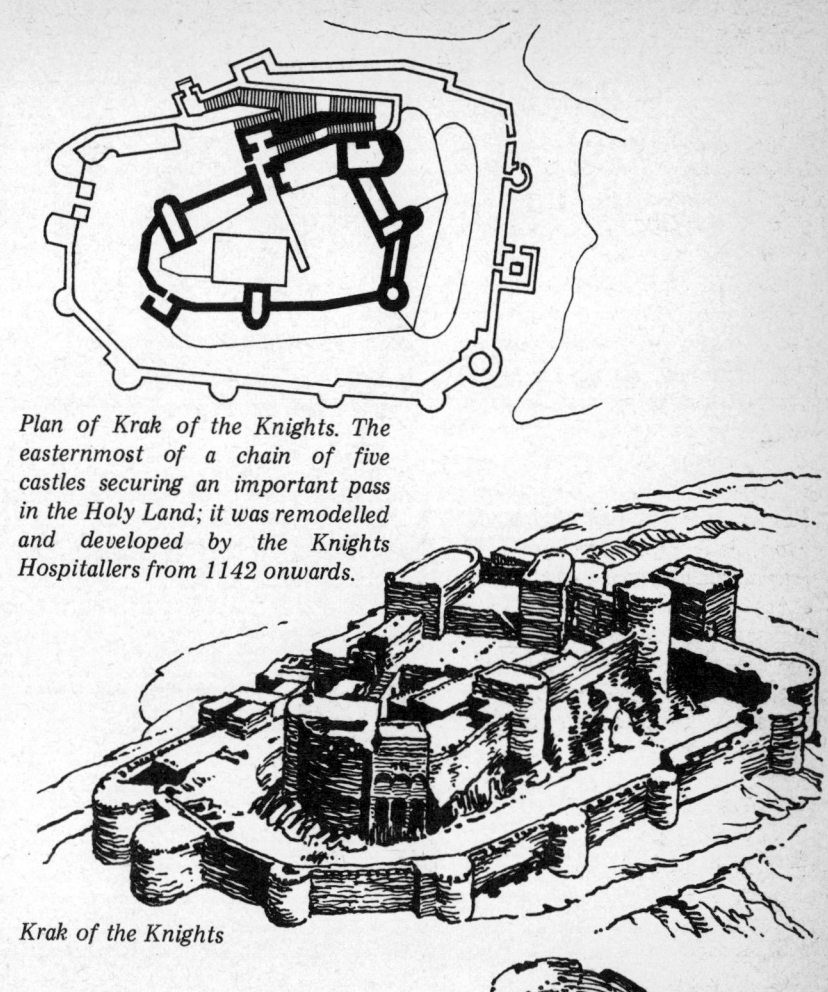

Plan of Krak of the Knights. The easternmost of a chain of five castles securing an important pass in the Holy Land; it was remodelled and developed by the Knights Hospitallers from 1142 onwards.

Krak of the Knights

Soane, originally fortified by the Greeks, was remodelled by the Crusaders in 1120. It had a powerful keep and thin outer curtain wall with rectangular towers.

Castle at Kyrenia, Cyprus. The castle at Kyrenia is concentrically planned.

CASTLES AND PALACES Byzantine and Medieval

The castles the Norman nobles built in 13th century Wales in their campaign to suppress the Welsh were inspired by the Crusader castles. When the Normans first invaded Wales their castles consisted of a mound of earth, a palissade, and a ditch. Then the 12th century Welsh princes began to build substantial castles; the mountains of south Wales slowed the Norman advance, while the hills contained the Welsh strongholds.

The most impressive castles were those built by Edward I from 1277 onwards in his long campaign against Llewelyn. They were built to control the sea and valley routes. Town walls were joined to the castles as a complete system of defence, as at Caernarvon and Chepstow. The round towers, seen first at Avila, and later developed in the Crusader castles, were incorporated in the new, concentrically planned castles, such as Caerphilly and Harlech.

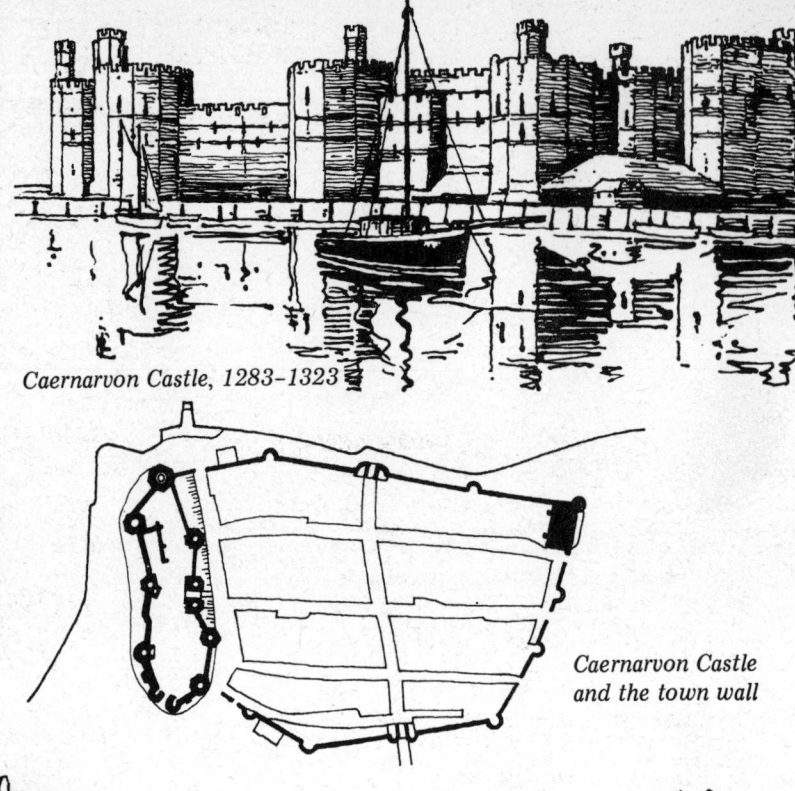

Caernarvon Castle, 1283–1323

Caernarvon Castle and the town wall

Caerphilly Castle, 1267–77

Harlech Castle, 1283–90

Chepstow Castle, begun in 1067

Pembroke Castle, begun in 1093

The Normans encouraged the development of planned townships adjoining a castle, as at Caernarvon and the 13th century fortified towns of Carcassonne and Aigues Mortes in France. Carcassonne has a double wall with fifty towers and a moat. The town was entered through five fortified gateways guarded by machicolations, drawbridge and portcullis. Inside the walls were narrow medieval streets, shops, houses, a cathedral and a castle.

The numerous fortified villages of the western Caucasus are more picturesque. They are similar to those of southern Morocco, and the medieval hill-city of San Gimignano, Italy. Each provided protection to peasants farming surrounding fields or provided shelter and security to traders travelling along the various commercial routes.

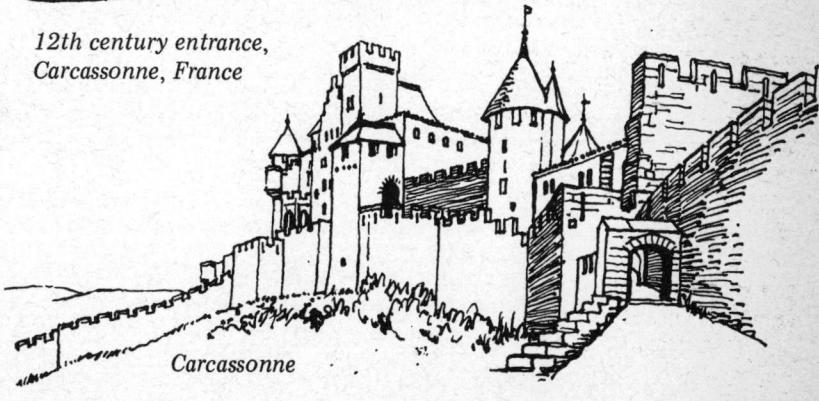

12th century entrance, Carcassonne, France

Carcassonne

13th century town walls and gateway, Aigues

Town gateway, Rhodes, 14th and 15th centuries

The medieval hill-city of San Gimignano, Italy, 13th and 14th centuries. Note the tall towers of the fortified houses. The towers were built by rival local families. Later fortified villages built in the western Caucasus are similar.

Fortified village, western Caucasus

CASTLES AND PALACES Byzantine and Medieval

Many of the early Norman manor houses in England were built of stone. They usually had some fortification, and for defensive purposes placed the main room, the hall, on the first floor.

At the beginning of the 13th century it was still necessary for buildings to have some defences even in the more settled areas of England, away from the troublesome border with Scotland. Licences to crenellate or fortify these manor houses were granted by Henry III. The concentrically planned castle, seen at its best at Beaumaris Castle (1295–1325) and Caerphilly Castle (1267–77), was in its heyday. The principle involved in building the concentric castles of the 13th and 14th centuries was that no part of the structure should be undefended or weaker than another. Cannon existed in 1326, and were almost certainly used in the battle of Crecy in 1346, but it was many years before they were the decisive element in battle.

By the mid-14th century the open field method of fighting had reduced the importance of castles. They were being replaced by forts and fortifications. The few castles that were built were designed more for comfort than war.

Concentrically planned castle

Stokesay Castle, Shropshire, 1285–1305

The keep of Dover Castle, 1180–86

Manor House, Boothby Pagnall, 1180

Deal Castle, 1540, built by Henry VIII

Bodiam Castle, Sussex, 1385

Herstmonceux Castle, Sussex, 1440

This concentric plan was followed by the quadrangular plan, as seen at Bodiam and Herstmonceux, castles of the late 14th and early 15th centuries. Castles and fortified residences were still built during the 15th century, although southern England was fairly settled and the need for such excessive fortifications had died. Inside, these new castles began to resemble palaces. Most relied largely on water for defence.

Henry VIII built a string of coastal castles in case of invasion from France, but the age of castle building had virtually ended.

Castles had been built in all European countries throughout the Middle Ages. The French castles were strongly fortified until after the ending of the Hundred Years War. Existing castles were adapted and extended as palaces.

The town halls of medieval Italy seem to continue the fortified tradition of the period, but much of this was purely symbolic, as the towns' fortifications were sufficiently strong. The noble families, well-protected within fortified towns or cities, built elaborate Gothic palaces like the Ca d'Oro in Venice.

Bran Castle, Rumania, 14th century

13th century Castle of Muiden, Holland

Kalmar Castle, Sweden, 14th century

Palazzo Ca d'Oro, Venice, 1421-36

Palazzo Vecchio, Florence, 1298-1344

Chateau at Chaumont, France, 1465-1515

Chateau de Pierrefonds, France, 1390-1400

CASTLES AND PALACES Classical

The Gothic palaces of late medieval Italy began to open the doors for new ideas. Their details were still very medieval, but the simpler shapes suggested a far greater purity and classical form. That form finally burst forth in the first palaces of the Italian Renaissance.

The Renaissance architects began to search for a new, purer order. They found such an order amongst the ruins of the Roman Empire. They reintroduced the classical Roman orders (column styles and details), which now became a characteristic feature of Renaissance Italy and, later, Europe. These orders, Tuscan, Doric, Ionic, Corinthian and Composite, were standardised by the great Renaissance architects Vignola, Palladio and Scamozzi. They attempted to copy the Roman grand manner of formal planning for its visual effects. Some of the new palaces retained a semi-fortress appearance. An example is the Palazzo Farnese, Caprarola, built by Vignola on a mountainside.

More typical palaces of 15th century Florence had an internal courtyard, similar to a medieval cloister, with an arcade supporting the upper storeys. The Roman palaces, on a larger scale, were simpler and more direct. In the still medieval atmosphere of Venice the palace was a blend between classic and medieval.

Palazzo Farnese, Rome, by Sangallo, 1515

Courtyard of the Ducal Palace, Urbino, by Luciano Laurano, 1444-82

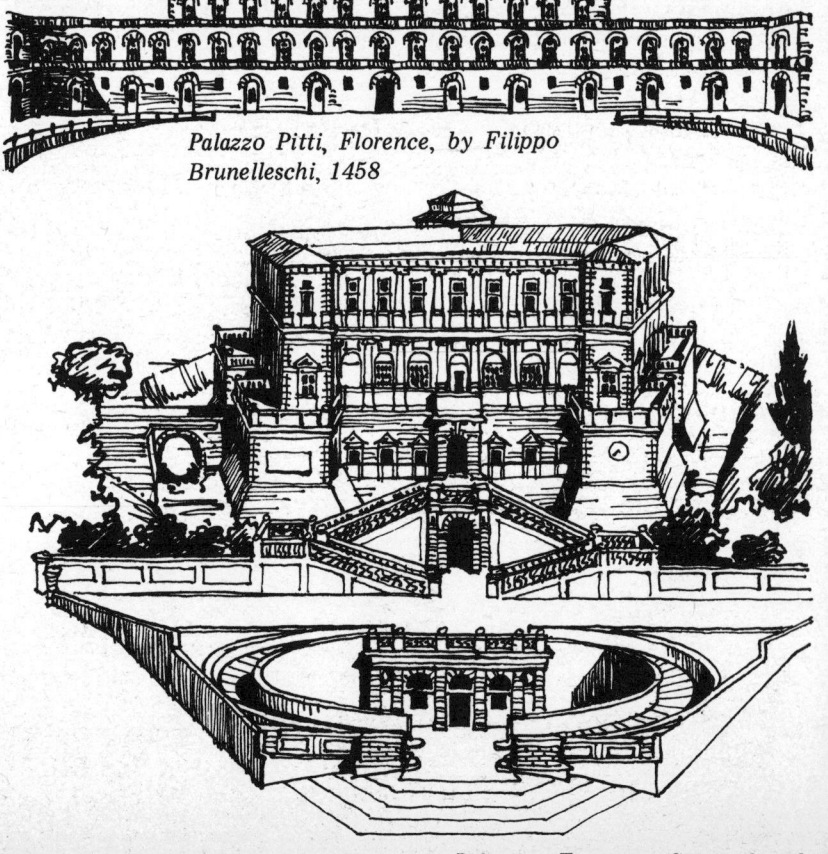

Palazzo Pitti, Florence, by Filippo Brunelleschi, 1458

Palazzo Grimani, Venice, by Michele Sanmichele, 1556

Palazzo Farnese, Caprarola, by Giacomo Vignola, 1547-49

In France many chateaux, such as Chambord (1519-47), were still semi-fortified, similar to a medieval concentric castle. The Gothic features had Renaissance details. Fontainbleau (1528-40) was originally a medieval castle. It was first converted to a manor house and then to a large chateau; eventually it became Napoleon's palace. The palace, unlike Chambord, depends for its effect, as did many later classical palaces, on the surrounding courts, formal gardens, terraces, lakes and radiating vistas.

It is the Palais de Versailles (1661-1756), with its enormous layout, that best sums up the period. Versailles was built round an old hunting chateau for Louis XIV by Le Vau, and was later extended by Jules Hardouin-Mansart. The magnificent gardens, laid out by Le Notre on axial lines designed to give vistas of avenues and water canals, were adorned with fountains, terraces and arbours. It is the exact opposite to Hadrian's villa at Tivoli. This is total coordinated design along a major axial line. It rivals that of the Forbidden City in Peking, only here there is a climax, the monumental palace.

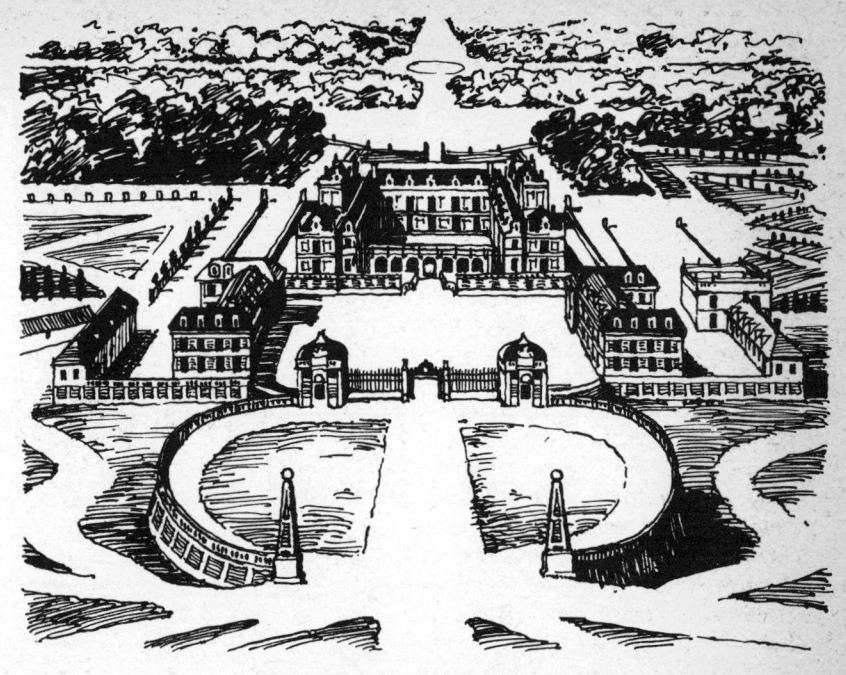

Palais de Versailles, by Le Vau, 1661–1756

Chateau de Chambord, by an Italian architect, Domenico da Cortona, 1519–47

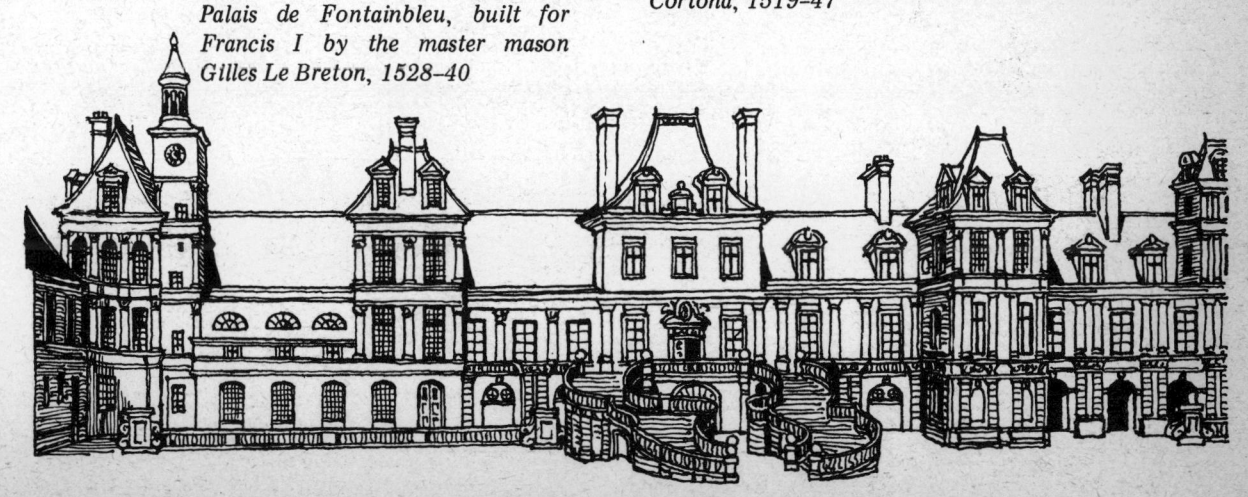

Palais de Fontainbleu, built for Francis I by the master mason Gilles Le Breton, 1528–40

CASTLES AND PALACES Classical

In the mid-16th century the scale of buildings began to increase enormously. The Escurial, 205 metres by 208 metres, was an austere group of buildings on a lonely site in Spain. It was almost as if another storey plus additional towers had been added to Diocletian's palace. The Escurial, like Ascheffenburg Castle in Germany and others throughout Europe, was still medieval in concept. It had immense, severe, fortified blocks with a tower at each corner. It was built around courtyards, the walls broken only by Renaissance windows.

Later castles and palaces were more classical in style. Many had projecting wings that curved around an immense entrance court. A characteristic feature of the early 18th century were the elegant domes that crowned the main hall centred along the axis. The hall was usually flanked by staircases. The main styles were now Baroque, Rococo and Neoclassical.

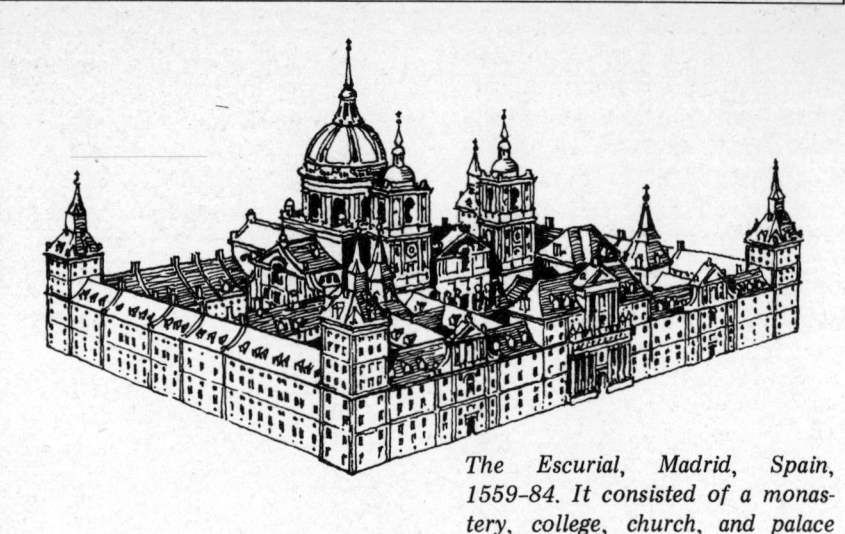

The Escurial, Madrid, Spain, 1559-84. It consisted of a monastery, college, church, and palace with state apartments.

Aschaffenburg Castle, Germany, 1605-14

The Marble Palace, St Petersburg, Russia, by Antonio Renaldi, 1768-72

Schloss Charlottenberg, Berlin, 1740-46

One of the first great Renaissance buildings in England was the Banqueting Hall, Whitehall, built by Inigo Jones. This was later to be part of what, if built, would have been one of the grandest Renaissance works in England, the Royal Palace designed by John Webb, Jones' talented student.

Vanbrugh treated the classical forms in a more monumental and exaggerated, or Baroque, manner when he designed Castle Howard and Blenheim Palace. These are large and imposing buildings. Blenheim has an entrance frontage of 261 metres, comprising the, by now, typical central block with portico and wings surrounding an immense court. Their size and cost soon made these gigantic houses obsolete. A more refined Palladian style of house took over. The style was developed by Burlington, Kent and Campbell, and can be seen in Holkham Hall, Chiswick House and Mereworth Castle.

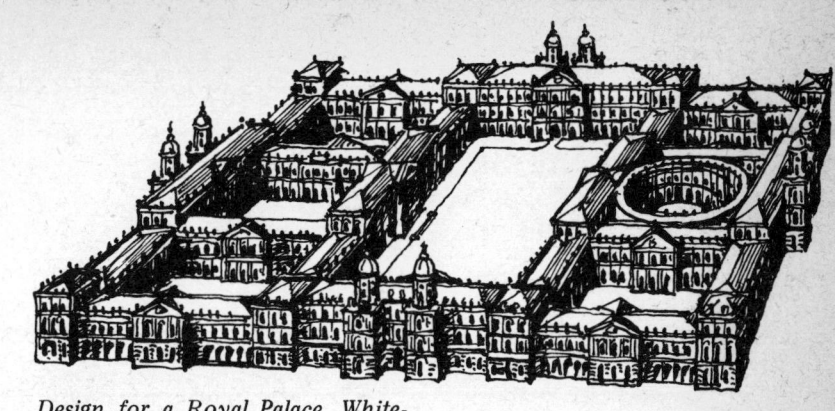

Design for a Royal Palace, Whitehall, London, by Inigo Jones 1619–21

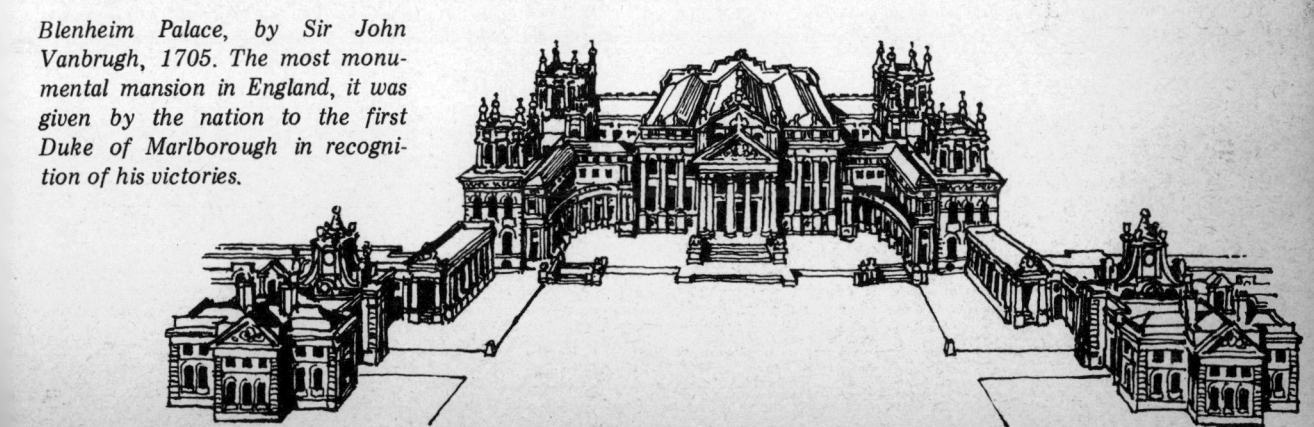

The Banqueting Hall, Whitehall by Inigo Jones

Castle Howard, Yorkshire by Sir John Vanbrugh, 1699–1712.

Blenheim Palace, by Sir John Vanbrugh, 1705. The most monumental mansion in England, it was given by the nation to the first Duke of Marlborough in recognition of his victories.

CASTLES AND PALACES The Modern World

By the 19th century the traditional castle and palace had lost their functions as defensive strongholds or imperial palaces, but the forms they developed were still to be seen. The Italian Renaissance palace was used by Barry for the design of two London clubs, the Reform and the Travellers' Club (1829-31). The remodelling of Highclere Castle was in the Elizabethan manor house style, and Cliveden, Buckinghamshire, resembles the monumental scale of the great Palazzo Farnese, Caprarola, Italy (1547-49). Some buildings were fashioned in the Greek or Roman style, others in the medieval. Everybody was sitting on the fence and wondering which way to go.

Reform Club, London, by Sir Charles Barry, 1837

Highclere Castle, Hampshire, remodelled by Sir Charles Barry, 1842-44

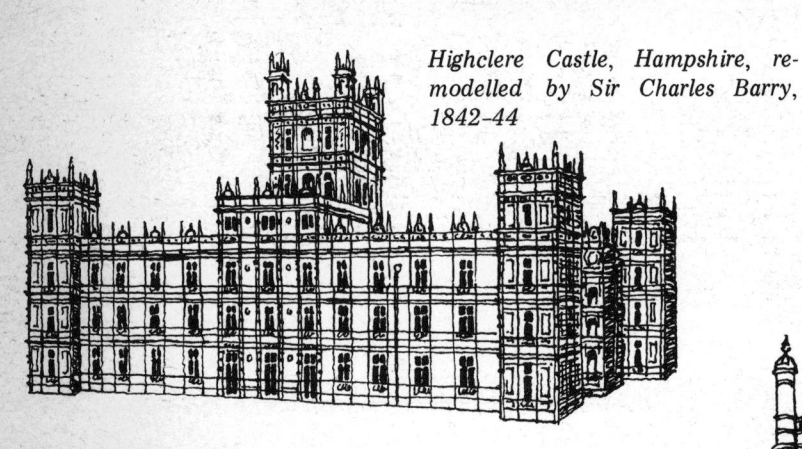

Cliveden, Buckinghamshire, rebuilt by Sir Charles Barry, 1850-51

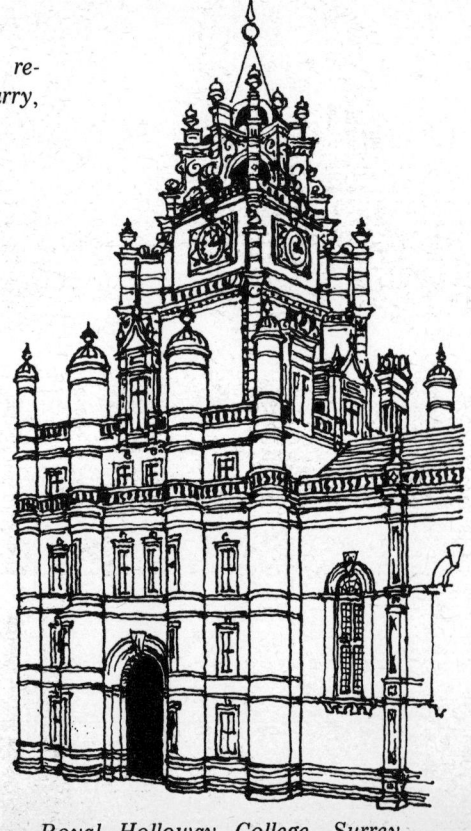

Royal Holloway College, Surrey, 1886. Now part of London University, it is an enormous rectangle in the French chateau style.

Castell Coch in Wales was the medieval fairytale castle, more real than the real thing. In India some seventy years later Le Corbusier did almost the same thing in the Millowners Association Building. It was less obvious, but there was the ramped entrance, and the suggestion of a drawbridge and portcullis. Louis Kahn, the great American architect, borrowed ideas from Hadrian's villa, Carcassonne and Piranesi's Rome in designing his 20th century buildings. The round towers of the synagogue planned for Philadelphia (1954) are reminiscent of the great walls of 11th century Avila, Spain, or the bold border castles built in 13th century Wales by Edward I. It was as if the symbolism of these medieval examples would give a strength and power to what might otherwise have been a fairly straightforward 20th century box. Kahn's design for the Richards Medical Research Laboratories for the University of Pennsylvania reminds you of the towers of San Gimignano.

Whatever Le Corbusier's and Kahn's reasons for choosing these forms, they did not include any form, no matter how attractive, unless it had some use. The towers and ramped entrances they used were as functional as those of the medieval castles. The towers of the laboratories at Philadelphia are for lifts and ventilation, and the round towers of the synagogue, with their slit windows, are for seminar rooms grouped around the sanctuary. The ramped entrance to the Millowners Association is the major gate to what, in a sense, is a castle. This is the headquarters of one of the most prominent Indian cotton millowners' associations. It was as if the Norman noble and his feudal castle had come full circle.

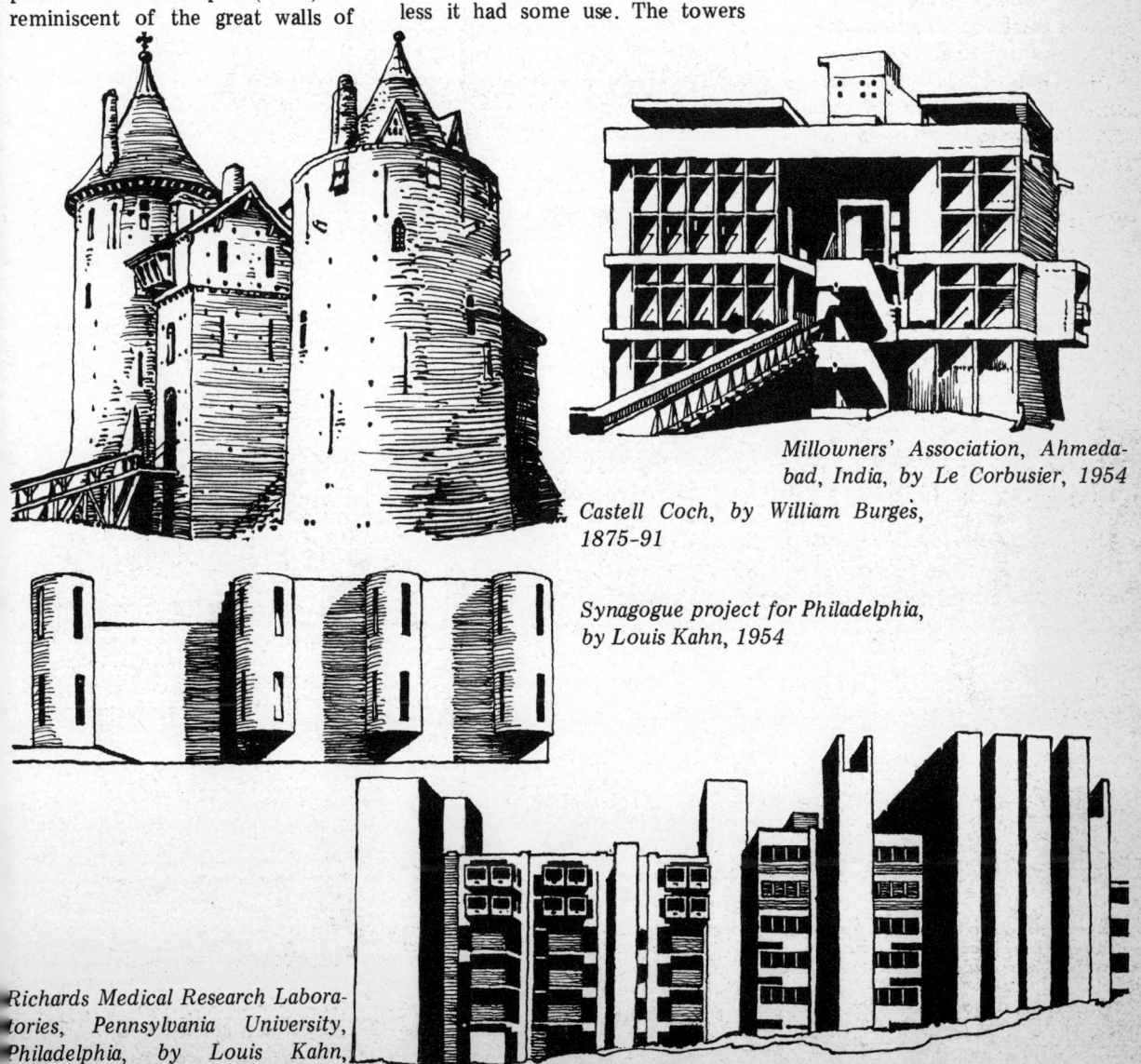

Millowners' Association, Ahmedabad, India, by Le Corbusier, 1954

Castell Coch, by William Burges, 1875-91

Synagogue project for Philadelphia, by Louis Kahn, 1954

Richards Medical Research Laboratories, Pennsylvania University, Philadelphia, by Louis Kahn, 1957-61

CASTLES AND PALACES Biographies

Sir Charles Barry (1795-1860)
English architect, designer of the Houses of Parliament. He was one of the most versatile of the leading early Victorian architects. He travelled in Greece, Italy, Egypt and Palestine between 1817 and 1820. Much of his work was in the Renaissance style, but his major building, the Houses of Parliament, was in the Tudor Gothic style. The external Perpendicular detail and all the internal detail are by Pugin.

Fillipo Brunelleschi (1377-1446)
Italian architect and sculptor. He is regarded as the founder of the Renaissance movement. He first visited Rome in 1402. His interest was more in Roman construction and engineering than in their aesthetics. In 1407 he won a competition for the completion of the cathedral in Florence with a dome. Other buildings designed by him include the churches of San Lorenzo (1420-5) and San Spirito (1444), and the Pitti Palace (c. 1435).

William Burges (1827-1881)
He trained originally as an engineer. He travelled extensively in France, Italy and Germany and was particularly interested in English and French Gothic architecture. His major works include Cork Cathedral (1826-70), and the remodelling of Castell Coch, near Cardiff (c. 1875).

Il Cronaca (1457-1508)
Italian architect and sculptor, born in Florence. He studied in Rome, then returned to Florence, where, in 1491, he was commissioned to complete the Strozzi Palace. Between 1495 and 1497 he took charge of the building of the Palazzo Vecchio.

Jules Hardoun-Mansart (1646-1708)
French architect. The grandnephew of the architect Francois Mansart, he took over the work at Versailles after Le Vau's death. He was appointed Royal Architect in 1675. His work owed much to Le Vau.

Inigo Jones (1573-1652)
English architect, theatrical designer, and architectural draftsman. He designed scenery for the court masques (1605-40) during the reigns of James I and Charles I. Following extensive travels in Italy, he began to introduce the mature Italian Renaissance (Palladian) architecture into England through such buildings as the Queen's House, Greenwich, the Banqueting Hall, Whitehall, and St Paul's, Covent Garden.

Louis Kahn (1901-1974)
American teacher, architect and urban designer. He studied and lived in Philadelphia. The building that made his reputation was the Richards Medical Research building for the University of Pennsylvania.

Le Corbusier (1887-1965)
French architect, writer, painter, sculptor, town planner. One of the greatest and most influential architects of the 20th century. He wrote several pioneering books on architecture and town planning as well as producing a remarkable range of buildings and projects. At first his work consisted of mainly small, elegant white houses. His later work consisted of the Unité d'Habitation at Marseille, various public buildings and town plans, including the design for the capital of the Punjab, Chandigarh.

Andre Le Notre (1613-1700)
Born in France, the son of a royal gardener. He was the greatest designer of formal parks and gardens. He studied painting and architecture as well as garden design. He worked mostly for Louis XIV. His masterpiece is the enormous park at Versailles (1662-90).

Louis Le Vau (1612-1670)
The leading Baroque architect in France. His masterpiece was the Chateau for Fouquet, Vaux-le-Vicomte (c. 1657). He was also in charge of the brilliant team of sculptors, decorators, painters and gardeners who created the Louis XIV style at Versailles.

Andrea Palladio (1518-1580)
Italian architect and writer. He was a major influence on architecture in England and Europe in the 17th and 18th centuries. He made an intensive study of the buildings of ancient Rome, which he later published in an influential book, *The Four Books of Architecture* (1570).

Antonio da Sangallo (1485-1546)
Born in Florence, he became the leading high Renaissance architect in Rome. He began as an architectural draftsman, working first for Bramante and then for Peruzzi. He became Raphael's assistant as architect to St Peter's in 1520. His masterpiece is the Palazzo Farnese, Rome.

Giacomo Barozzi da Vignola (1507-1573)
After the death of Michelangelo he became the leading architect in Rome. The Palazzo Farnese, Caprarola (1550), which he was asked to complete, was his first important work. The pentagonal plan had been started by Peruzzi. The Gesù, Rome (1568), his most influential building, has probably had a greater influence on architecture than any other church designed in the last 400 years. He was architect to St Peter's (1567-73), where he continued the work of Michelangelo.